SPIRIT-FILLED
TEACHING

SPIRIT-FILLED TEACHING

THE POWER OF THE HOLY SPIRIT IN YOUR MINISTRY

ROY B. ZUCK

CHARLES R. SWINDOLL, GENERAL EDITOR

WORD PUBLISHING

NASHVILLE

A Thomas Nelson Company

SPIRIT-FILLED TEACHING
Swindoll Leadership Library

Published in association with Dallas Theological Seminary (DTS):
General Editor: Charles R. Swindoll
Managing Editor: Roy B. Zuck

The theological opinions expressed by the author are not necessarily the
official position of Dallas Theological Seminary.

Zuck, Roy B.
Spirit-filled teaching : The power of the Holy Spirit in your ministry /
Roy B. Zuck ; Charles R. Swindoll, general editor.
p.   cm.—(Swindoll leadership library)
Includes bibliographical references.

ISBN 0-8499-1560-0

1. Holy Spirit. 2. Clergy—Office.
3. Pastoral theology. 4. Christian education—Philosophy. I. Swindoll,
Charles R. II. Title. III. Series

BT123.Z83   1998
268'.01—dc21   98-15090
                                                                                  CIP

Printed in the United States of America
98 99 00 01 02 03 04 05 06 BVG 9 8 7 6 5 4 3 2

CONTENTS

❧

Good Study of Role of H.S.

Good Principles of Interpreting Scripture! How do we Guard one person interpretat. af that of another? >

FOREWORD

I HAVE ALWAYS MARVELED at Jesus' ability to teach with authority, power, and effectiveness. His messages were *not* dusty, rusty homilies that produced spiritual drowsiness and lethargy in an audience. Nor did He speak with a self-inflated eloquence that was long on style and short on substance. No, Jesus taught in a down-to-earth way that gripped the mind and heart, grabbing the full attention of His audience.

The Gospel of Matthew presents at least part of the reason for Jesus' ability to captivate and confront an audience. At the beginning of His ministry, heaven opened and "the Spirit of God descending like a dove" came on Him (Matt. 3:16). The descent of God's Spirit was followed by a "wilderness experience" where Jesus successfully used God's Word to overcome Satan's temptations (4:1–11). The possession of God's Spirit, the knowledge of God's Word, and the victorious response to Satan's temptations prepared Jesus to be an effective teacher.

These events are followed by "the Sermon on the Mount" (Matt. 5–7), one of the longest recorded messages by Jesus. How effective was He? The inspired record tells us, "When Jesus had finished saying these things, the crowds were amazed at his teaching, because he taught as one who had authority, and not as their teachers of the law" (7:28–29).

How can we teach with the same power, clarity, and effectiveness? The answer does not lie in human methods and techniques, helpful as they are. As Dr. Roy Zuck clearly demonstrates in this volume, effective teaching is absolutely dependent on the ministry of the Holy Spirit. Only God's Spirit can bring about true change in the lives of those whom we teach.

Zuck tackles some of the often neglected—but vital—issues on this key ministry of the Holy Spirit. What is the Holy Spirit's role in teaching? How do I know if I have the biblical "gift" of teaching? What part does the Holy Spirit play in enabling me to interpret God's Word? These questions are answered with helpful insight.

Zuck also rivets our attention on the centrality of God's Word in all effective teaching. The Bible is the authority for all Christian education, and he shows his mastery of God's Word throughout the book. Simply put, the man practices what he preaches.

Whether you are teaching a small class of preschoolers or preaching to a large congregation, your effectiveness will be directly related to the work of the Holy Spirit in your life as you handle God's Word. Before turning to the first chapter in this volume, pause and ask God to allow His Spirit to open your mind to the truth in these pages. Seek His insight, understanding, and guidance so you, too, can teach "as one who had authority."

—CHARLES R. SWINDOLL
General Editor

PREFACE

To MANY PEOPLE, Christian education means methods, materials, organization, and programs. Thus conceived, Christian education seems like something foisted on Christianity and foreign to anything theological or spiritual.

Of course the work of Christian education does involve methods, materials, organization, and programs. But it is more than these. Simply defined, evangelical Christian education is the Christ-centered, Bible-based, student-related process of communicating God's written Word through the power of the Holy Spirit, for the purpose of guiding individuals to know and grow in Christ.

Defined in this way, evangelical Christian education is a theological discipline—a work to be rooted deeply in and derived squarely from theological concepts and biblical truths. And it is a divine-human task, in which born-again teachers face the thrilling opportunity of cooperating with God, the Holy Spirit, as "workers together with Him" (2 Cor. 6:1, KJV).

The purpose of this study is to demonstrate the need for the ministry of the Holy Spirit in our teaching and to discuss how the Spirit works in the various phases of the teaching-learning process. It is written for teachers and other educational workers in local churches, and also for those engaged in Christian teaching in educational institutions on elementary, secondary, and higher levels and in other church-related agencies.

I trust that this book will help bridge the rift that sometimes exists between theology and Christian education, and that it will inspire teachers to give God's Spirit His rightful place in their educational ministries—and thus enjoy the divine dynamics of teaching!

This book was first published in 1963, under the title *The Holy Spirit in Your Teaching,* and was revised in 1984, and again now in 1998.

I thank my wife, Dottie, for encouraging me in this work, and for her sacrificial assistance that helped make this book possible.

May God bless those teachers everywhere who, being taught by Him, faithfully commit God's precious Word to their students, so that they, in turn, may "also be qualified to teach others" (2 Tim. 2:2).

PART ONE
THE BIBLICAL DOCTRINE OF THE HOLY SPIRIT AS A TEACHER

What does the Bible say about the Holy Spirit as a Teacher? How does His teaching ministry relate to His other ministries? How are certain difficult passages about the Spirit's place in teaching to be understood?

Knowing what the Bible teaches about the divine Teacher Himself will help teachers know better how to depend on and cooperate with Him as they teach God's Word.

CHAPTER 1
POWER IN YOUR TEACHING

I OFTEN WONDER if I'm getting through to my pupils."

"Why do I seem to have so few results in my Bible teaching? I seem to be getting nowhere."

"I feel that I'm making little or no spiritual headway in my class. Apparently my students aren't growing in the Lord."

Do these statements reflect your feelings as a Bible teacher? Do you sense that you lack spiritual effectiveness?

WHY HEARERS ONLY?

Why do so many in churches today seem unchallenged and unchanged by Bible teaching? Why are many children anxious for their Sunday-school classes to be over? Why is it that many young people would call Bible studies "Dullsville"? Why do many adults respond to Bible classes with yawns, ho-hums, and "so what's"?

Must we be content with lack of spiritual growth and maturity, with the absence of Christlike living? Can we do nothing to bridge the chasm that seems to exist between students' knowledge of the truth and their practice of it?

The teaching—and the learning—of God's Word ought to be an interesting, exuberant adventure. Communicating God's precious truth ought to result in transformed lives, and in pupils being "doers of the

Word and not merely hearers" (James 1:22, NASB). But too often Bible classes are lifeless, uninteresting, the essence of boredom.

Lois LeBar asks, "How do our young people leave their Sunday School classrooms on Sunday morning? With eyes sparkling with new vision and insight? With serious determination to practice the will of God? With chin up ready to face an unbelieving world in the power of the Spirit? With deep questions about God Himself? Too often they are glad for release from a dull, boring session."[1]

WHAT ARE THE DYNAMICS OF BIBLE TEACHING?

More pastors, teachers, youth leaders, and other church workers are increasingly aware of the fact that Christianity is, to a large extent, educational. Church leaders are seeing that a balanced, coordinated, educational church program can help dispel student disinterest. Employing appropriate teaching techniques and using suitable instructional materials can help make teaching more exciting.

But these factors—important as they are—cannot, in themselves, guarantee teaching power and effectiveness.

Secular educators use these educational factors to good advantage, but one cannot say therefore that secular education possesses spiritual vitality. And even theologically liberal religious educators seek to use the best in teaching procedures and materials. But evangelicals would not concede that liberal religious educators know much of the spiritual reality so necessary to transform individuals' lives toward Christlikeness.

There must be something else that guarantees spiritual effectiveness in Bible teaching—and which at the same time makes evangelical Christian education distinctive from secular teaching and liberal religious education.

The three indispensable factors that make Christian education dynamic, and at the same time distinctive, are (1) the centrality of God's written revelation, (2) the necessity of regeneration, and (3) the ministry of the Holy Spirit. These are the dynamics of Christian education. The presence and functioning of these three together make up a distinctive education, from the evangelical standpoint. To seek to have

Christian education without the Word of God is to extricate the basic core of the curriculum. Unregenerate teachers cannot communicate, in the full sense of the word, Christian truths which they themselves do not know experientially. And the Holy Spirit's work is necessary for spiritual enablement in every phase of teaching and learning.

THE CENTRALITY OF REVELATION

Without the Bible as the foundation and core of the curriculum, there can be no true Christian education. An adequate philosophy of Christian education must incorporate the basic concept of God's revelation of Himself to finite human beings through His written Word, the Bible.

Because of their sinful, depraved condition, the unsaved are spiritually dead and do not know God (Rom. 3:10–23; 1 Cor. 2:14; Eph. 2:1–2). Therefore God has revealed Himself to people in various ways: in creation (which is referred to as "general revelation" and which reveals God's wisdom, power, and glory); in direct revelation (especially, in Old Testament times, through dreams, visions, and the spoken word); in miracles; in Christ, the eternal, living Word (John 1:1, 14; 14:9–11); and in the written Word, God's scriptural revelation. Scripture is itself revelation.[2] "While the process of revelation is broader than the Bible, the content of special revelation is for us identical with the biblical message."[3]

In evangelical Christian education the Bible is our supreme and final authority, the infallible guide to faith and practice, for three reasons.

First, this revelation is from God. Since He has revealed Himself in permanent, written form, we need not search further for a source of knowledge about Him and a means of experiencing Him. His revelation is divinely inspired by the Holy Spirit (2 Tim. 3:16; 2 Pet. 1:20–21) and is therefore infallible and authoritative.

The Bible is our content—*what* we are to teach. It is essential to any ministry that seeks to teach others God's ways and will.

Second, God's written Word is basic in Christian education because it is the means of imparting divine life (we are "born again . . . through . . . the Word of God," 1 Pet. 1:23), and it is the source of Christian nurture and growth (we are to "crave pure spiritual milk, so that by it [we] may

3

grow up," 2:2). A valid Christian experience (whether birth into the Christian life—regeneration; or growth within the Christian life—edification) cannot be obtained or maintained apart from the Scriptures. Life attitudes can hardly be changed apart from a knowledge of the Bible, an awareness of biblical ideals, and a scripturally based worldview.[4] "Factual Bible knowledge in the life of a Christian is the necessary foundation on which the Holy Spirit must build."[5]

If Christian experience or knowledge of God is sought from sources other than biblical revelation, then Christian education is nothing more than a humanistic, man-centered "religious" education. In true Christian education the Bible is the objective body of truth to which the experiences of students are to be related and by which students' experiences are to be affected.

Third, scriptural revelation provides a standard by which our experiences may be measured. Without the Bible as the foundation of Christian education, how can we measure whether our learners are growing spiritually? Omit the Bible, and you have no objective basis or ground of evaluation by which to judge the validity of spiritual experiences. Without the Bible, teachers and students are left to subjective, self-imposed standards. But with God's revelation as the standard, unsaved students are challenged to accept Christ as their Savior, and those who know the Lord are challenged to lead lives of holiness (1 Thess. 5:23; 1 Pet. 1:15) and to mature into Christlikeness (Rom. 8:29; 2 Cor. 3:18; Eph. 4:12–13).

Therefore the place of written revelation is essential to education that is distinctly Christian. The Bible is the infallible, objective body of truth essential to the transformation of lives, first in salvation and then in Christ-centered living.

THE NECESSITY OF REGENERATION

Only teachers who are regenerated by the Spirit of God (Titus 3:5) and are thus born into God's family qualify as Christian teachers.

To neglect this distinctive is to destroy the lines of demarcation between mere religious education and true Christian education, between liberal religious teaching and evangelical Christian teaching. Some leaders say that teachers only need to be religious-minded and have some kind of nebulously defined faith in God.

Others are giving more attention to the sinful nature of man, the need for God's grace, and the reconciling work of Christ. While these educators seem more concerned that their teaching be theologically oriented, these emphases have done little to cause them to stress the new birth as a requisite for Christian teaching.

Teaching, to be distinctly Christian, must be conducted by persons who have been redeemed through faith in Jesus Christ and who thus have a personal relationship with Him. Without the living reality of salvation through God's grace, a teacher is not a Christian, and his or her teaching is not Christian teaching in the truest sense. This is true for several reasons.

First, the aim of Christian education necessitates born-again teachers. The transformation of lives, the growth of Christian personalities, the nurturing of learners toward conformity to the will of God demand that teachers possess high spiritual objectives. As Findley Edge has stated, *"A personal experience of conversion is the only adequate foundation and the only significant motivation for Christian growth."*[6]

Second, the nature of Christian teaching demands born-again instructors. Christian teaching is a divine calling, not simply a secular vocation. It is a God-ordained ministry in which divinely appointed persons communicate the truths of a divinely inspired Book, to help students lead Christ-honoring lives.

Since the entire process is a divine one, only those who are divinely regenerated by God's Spirit qualify to engage in this ministry. An unsaved person, even though religious, does not know God and therefore is incapable of communicating the truth and will of God to others.

Third, the influence of teachers' lives demands that teachers know Christ in salvation. The life, words, actions, attitudes, convictions, and objectives of a teacher influence his or her students. A teacher who does not know Christ as Savior is unable to influence students with the realities of his own Christian life, because he has none. God's plan is to teach through regenerated personalities whom He indwells.

THE MINISTRY OF THE HOLY SPIRIT

Christian education demands using the Word of God and only born-again instructors, but even these do not guarantee that Christian teaching will be spiritually effective.

The Holy Spirit, working through the Word of God, is the spiritual dynamic for Christian living. If the Holy Spirit is not at work through the teacher and through the written Word of God, then our teaching remains virtually ineffective and is little different from secular teaching. Could this explain why so much of our teaching is dull and falls on deaf ears and hard hearts? Andrew Murray stresses the sterility of Christianity apart from the energizing of the Holy Spirit: "The reason that there is so much Bible reading and teaching which has no power to elevate and sanctify the life is simply this: it is not truth which has been revealed and received through the Holy Spirit."[7]

James Murch very pointedly decries the insipid condition of much Christian teaching: "The average church school of our day overlooks the divine element in Christian education. It is a slave to cold propositions, to methods and programs which are purely intellectual in concept. Thus it lacks divine warmth and passion. . . . It fails to give the spiritual dynamic for Christian living."[8]

But why is the Holy Spirit's ministry so essential in a process that is basically educational? Can't regenerate teachers using a Bible-structured curriculum be known as Christian educators? If a prepared teacher follows sound pedagogical principles, uses proper teaching methods, is interested in his students, and operates within a Bible-based curriculum, doesn't that constitute true Christian teaching? Emphatically no! A number of facts make the ministry of the Holy Spirit essential to dynamic Bible teaching.

First, the work of God's Spirit in the lives of regenerate teachers is needed so that they may be effective instruments in the hands of God. God's servants must be properly adjusted to the Spirit of God. The powerless, ineffective living of many believers attests to the fact that being rightly related to Christ (in salvation) does not necessarily mean being rightly related to the Holy Spirit (in spirituality). Salvation and spirituality are two different matters. A person is saved when he or she places faith in Christ; one is "spiritual" when he or she is yielded to and filled with God's Spirit (Gal. 5:16; Eph. 5:18). One who is saved may at once yield to God and be spiritual; but too often after salvation, Christians lead carnal lives, unyielded to God.

Effectiveness in service, after we are saved, depends on our being yielded to the Holy Spirit. Service done merely by our own efforts—including even teaching the Bible—is of little avail.

Too often Christian teachers fail to allow for the Spirit's guidance, enablement, and enlightenment as they prepare and as they teach. Thus they are hardly different from unsaved teachers in secular education who know of no such available source of enablement. Unregenerate teachers have no spiritual resources; Christian teachers have spiritual resources but often fail to use them!

How can your students be led to experience fellowship with God if you are not walking in fellowship with the Lord? Dynamic Spirit-filled living on your part can help encourage those you teach to likewise enjoy the Holy Spirit's filling.

This is not to suggest, however, that all you need for effective teaching is to lead a holy life. You must also follow principles of learning and teaching (discussed in chapters 11 and 12). Effective teaching of spiritual truths for spiritual growth is not an either/or—either depending fully on the Holy Spirit to the neglect of pedagogical procedures or, as Lee suggests,[9] depending fully on educational procedures to the neglect of the Holy Spirit.

Second, the Holy Spirit's ministry is needed so that the Holy Spirit and the written Word of God work in conjunction. "Bible knowledge in the heart of a Christian must be acted on by the Holy Spirit in order to produce Christian conduct."[10]

Those who object to this thought say that the Bible is an energized, animated Book, able to redeem, empower, and enlighten by itself, without the accompanying ministry of the Holy Spirit.

True, the Bible is a living, powerful Book. Twice in Scripture—in Hebrews 4:12 and 1 Peter 1:23—the Word of God is said to be "living." And twice in Scripture the Word of God is said to be "active" (Heb. 4:12; 1 Thess. 2:13). Hebrews 4:12 contains the adjective "active," which comes from the Greek word *energēs*, "operative or effective." In 1 Thessalonians 2:13 the Word of God, Paul wrote, "is at work in you who believe." The words "is at work" translate *energeitai*. This verb, "to be operative, active, effective," is related to the adjective *energēs*.

Being God-breathed and verbally inspired, the Bible has divine life resident in it. Thus it has power to generate faith (Ps. 19:7; Rom. 10:17; 2 Tim. 3:15; James 1:18; 1 Pet. 1:23), to sanctify and nurture (John 17:17–19; Acts 20:32; Eph. 5:26; 1 Pet. 2:2), and to enlighten (Ps. 119:105, 130; 2 Tim. 3:16). Its supernatural power and animating vitality must not be underestimated. In fact, this is one reason scriptural revelation stands as an essential divine element in Christian education.

However, when we consider all of Scripture, it becomes evident that the Holy Spirit and the Word of God operate together. The Holy Spirit's ministry is essential for any proper reception of the truth (1 Cor. 2:12–15; Eph. 1:17–18). The Holy Spirit, along with the Word, is said to regenerate (John 3:5–7; Titus 3:5), to sanctify (2 Thess. 2:13; 1 Peter 1:2), and to enlighten (John 14:26; 16:13; 1 Cor. 2:10–15).

Therefore it is obvious that "the written Word . . . is always indissolubly joined with the power of the Holy Spirit."[11] However, two questions must be considered. What is the relationship between the Word and the Spirit? Why isn't the Word of God effective by itself?

An answer may be obtained by distinguishing between the "resident life" of the Scriptures themselves and their "effectiveness." That is, the Bible has life, but it does not always beget life. Its effectiveness is evident only when the Holy Spirit is at work in it. "When a man hears the Word of God and believes it, in his heart the Holy Spirit makes it life."[12]

This is verified by both experience and scriptural revelation. Not all who hear the Word believe (for example, John 10:25; 12:47–48; Acts 7:57–59; 17:5, 32). Many who hear the truth are not regenerated because the Spirit of God has not so used the Word as to bring about their salvation. Hodge points out that for the Word of God to regenerate, the Holy Spirit must supernaturally (and simultaneously, it should be added) remove the spiritual blindness of unbelievers to enable them to receive the saving power of the Word (2 Cor. 4:3–4; John 16:7–1 1).[13]

Also many believers are not growing by means of the Word—though they hear the Word—because their sinful living prohibits the Holy Spirit from making the Word and its truths operative in their lives (1 Cor. 3:1–3; Heb. 5:12–14).

The impact of the Word depends on the Holy Spirit's ministry. Ronald Wallace states that "the Word of God can have no efficacy unless at the same time the Holy Spirit works in the hearts of the hearers, creating faith and making men's minds open to receive the Word."[14] Commenting on our receptivity to the Bible, John Calvin wrote, "The heavenly doctrine proves to be useful . . . to us only so far as the Spirit both forms our minds to understand it and our hearts to submit to its yoke."[15]

Therefore in both salvation and Christian living the Holy Spirit's ministry is essential. Though the Bible is "living and active" (that is, alive and at work, Heb. 4:12), it does not accomplish what God intends unless the Spirit's ministry is also involved. The Scriptures accomplish their purposes to the extent that learners appropriate the Word by the Holy Spirit. The question is not that of the inherent power of the Word— that is granted. The question is whether the Holy Spirit is appropriating the Word to individuals' lives.

Christian teachers cannot afford to neglect the place of the Spirit's ministry, as they seek to communicate the Bible to students and as students seek to appropriate it.

As Griffith Thomas wrote, "In all Christian work, there are three elements absolutely indispensable: the Spirit of God as the power, the Word of God as the message, and the man of God as the instrument. The Spirit of God uses the message by means of the man."[16] These three emphases—the Holy Spirit; God's written revelation, the Bible; and regenerate teachers—are basic to an adequate approach to Christian teaching. To neglect them, or any one of them, is to fail to have true Christian education. Only with all three can teachers begin to experience something of the divine dynamics of Christian teaching.

TO THINK ABOUT

1. Do you sometimes sense that your students are not responsive to God's Word? What do you think contributes to this lack of living out the truths they know?

2. Why is it important for students to know the Bible? What consequences may stem from a person's life if he or she is ignorant of the Word of God?

3. Why must a person be saved in order to teach effectively? Can you think of someone who is not regenerate and who has attempted to teach the Bible?

4. What impact did this fact have on his or her teaching?

5. Have you experienced times in your teaching when you sensed you were not adequately depending on the Holy Spirit to guide and empower you? What effect did this have on those sessions?

CHAPTER 2
THE TITLES OF THE HOLY SPIRIT
AS A TEACHER

When Paul arrived in Ephesus on his third missionary journey, he met some people who said, "We have not even heard that there is a Holy Spirit" (Acts 19:2). Unfortunately that may also be true of some Christians today. Or if they have heard about Him, they know little about who He is and what He does.

I have found that true in teaching adults in Sunday-school classes; a few can cite only a handful of the many ministries of the Holy Spirit. The Bible mentions the following works of the third person of the Godhead:

- Creates
- Inspires
- Illumines
- Restrains
- Convicts
- Regenerates
- Baptizes
- Seals
- Anoints
- Indwells
- Fills
- Empowers
- Commands
- Sanctifies
- Assures
- Witnesses
- Intercedes
- Commissions
- Encourages
- Controls
- Strengthens
- Counsels
- Helps
- Protects
- Produces fruit
- Reveals
- Teaches
- Declares

- Guides
- Comforts
- Reminds
- Gives wisdom, hope, joy

Besides the many works by the Holy Spirit, He also has many titles. John Walvoord lists thirty-six titles found in the Bible.[1] Of these, at least six relate to His work of teaching: Spirit of wisdom and of understanding, Spirit of counsel and of power, Spirit of knowledge and of the fear of the Lord, Spirit of truth, Counselor, Spirit of wisdom and revelation. Examining these titles can help us see how God the Holy Spirit is involved in our teaching ministries.

SPIRIT OF WISDOM AND OF UNDERSTANDING

"Spirit of wisdom and of understanding" is the first of three pairs of titles ascribed to the Holy Spirit in Isaiah 11:2. Christ, the "Shoot . . . from the stump of Jesse" (11:1), was equipped by God's Spirit for His great earthly ministry (61:1; Matt. 3:16). The Spirit of God, Isaiah predicted, "will rest [literally, 'settle down'] on Him" (Isa. 11:1), and as a result, Christ possessed wisdom, understanding, counsel, power, knowledge, and the fear of the Lord. These gifts are given by the Spirit to Christ, and apparently are given to some extent by the Spirit to Christian teachers today.

Only one Spirit descended on Christ (the verb "will rest" is singular), but the Holy Spirit is designated by several titles because He bestows several benefits.

"The first pair [wisdom and understanding] relates to the intellectual life, the second [counsel and power] to the practical life, and the third [knowledge and the fear of the Lord] to the direct relation to God."[2] The Hebrew word for "wisdom" (ḥokmâ) suggests skill, experience, or expertise (cf. wisdom in relation to skill in Exodus 28:3), and the word for "understanding" (bînâ) suggests discernment and perception. It is interesting that a form of the Hebrew word for "understanding" is translated "teachers" in Ezra 8:16 (NASB) and "men of learning" (NIV) in referring to Joiarib and Elnathan. They helped others gain insight or discernment.

12

SPIRIT OF COUNSEL AND OF POWER

The title "Spirit of counsel and of power" in Isaiah 11:2 depicts His ability to impart the gift of forming proper plans (or giving proper advice) and of carrying them out with physical energy. The word *counsel* suggests the ability to provide good advice, and the word *might* suggests the ability to carry out that counsel. The Holy Spirit enabled Christ to carry on His earthly teaching ministry by supplying Him with counsel and energy. The Spirit seeks to provide similar counsel and insight, might and strength to Christian teachers today.

SPIRIT OF KNOWLEDGE
AND OF THE FEAR OF THE LORD

The Holy Spirit also supplied Christ with "knowledge and the fear of the Lord." Though "the fear of the Lord is the beginning [starting point and essence] of knowledge" (Prov. 1:7), the fact that this title occurs last in Isaiah 11:2 suggests that the fear of the Lord is also the end result of knowledge. True knowledge must begin with and result in reverence for God, in recognition of His lordship and sovereignty. The Holy Spirit seeks to supply Christian teachers with both knowledge and godly reverence, two inseparable requisites for teaching God's Word effectively.

From these three titles of the Holy Spirit in Isaiah 11:2 it is clear that Christ was specially endowed by the Holy Spirit with prudence, discernment, counsel, strength, knowledge, and reverence for God the Father. These can be the portion of born-again instructors today too as we depend on the Spirit for His enabling.

SPIRIT OF TRUTH

The title "Spirit of truth" occurs three times in the Bible and only in John's Gospel: John 14:17; 15:26; 16:13. Some writers suggest this title means that the Holy Spirit is "the true Spirit" or "the truthful Spirit." Others say the title indicates that the Holy Spirit bears witness to Christ, who is the truth (14:6).[3]

But these three verses, particularly John 16:13, support the idea that the title "Spirit of truth" refers to the Holy Spirit as the *Source* of truth. "When He, the Spirit of truth, comes, He will guide you into all truth" (16:13). And closely related to this is the thought that He is the Spirit of truth because He communicates and *applies* the truth to believers' lives. The Spirit can apply the truth to your students' lives because He is the Source of truth. Many commentators hold this view. For example, Lange states that "He is the Spirit of truth, inasmuch as He makes objective truth subjective in believers."[4]

You may present God's truth ("Your word is truth," John 17:17) to others, but only the Spirit of truth can impart and apply that truth personally.

COUNSELOR

"Counselor" is the NIV translation of the word "Paraclete," an English transliteration of the Greek *paraklētos*. This Greek word occurs five times in the New Testament, all in John's writings: John 14:16, 26; 15:26; 16:7; and 1 John 2:1. In the Gospel of John the word speaks of the Holy Spirit; in 1 John it is used of Christ. In translating the word *paraklētos* in the Gospel of John, the KJV has "Comforter," the NASB and the NKJV have "Helper," and the NIV has "Counselor." In 1 John the word *paraklētos*, used of Christ, is rendered "Advocate" by the KJV and the NASB, and "Defense" by the NIV. The verses in the Gospel of John in the NIV read as follows:

> And I will ask the Father, and He will give you another Counselor to be with you forever—the Spirit of truth. The world cannot accept Him, because it neither sees Him nor knows Him. But you know Him, for He lives with you and will be in you. (John 14:16–17)

> But the Counselor, the Holy Spirit, whom the Father will send in My name, will teach you all things, and will remind you of everything I have said to you. (14:26)

When the Counselor comes, whom I will send to you from the Father, the Spirit of truth who goes out from the Father, He will testify about Me. (15:26)

But I tell you the truth: It is for your good that I am going away. Unless I go away, the Counselor will not come to you; but if I go, I will send Him to you. When He comes, He will convict the world of guilt in regard to sin and righteousness and judgment. (16:7–8)

These verses indicate that the Paraclete was given and sent by God the Father (14:26), proceeds from the Father (15:26), and was sent by God the Son (15:26; 16:7). He came to be with the disciples forever (14:16), to indwell them (14:17), to teach them and to remind them of Christ's teachings (14:26), and to testify about Christ (15:26). He is identified as the Holy Spirit (14:26). The world will not accept Him (14:17), and He will convict the world (16:8).

Christ said the Spirit would be "another" Paraclete, another like Himself who would take His place. "Another" is the Greek word *allos*, "another of the same kind," not *heteros*, "another of a different kind." This suggests that Christ too was a Paraclete. Just as Christ is a person, so is the Spirit. Just as Christ was sent by the Father (3:17; 16:28), so the Spirit was sent by the Father (14:17; 14:26; 15:26). Just as Christ came (18:37), so the Spirit came (14:26). Just as Christ came in the Father's name (5:43), so the Spirit came in the Father's name (14:26). Just as the Father gave Christ (3:16), so the Father gave the Spirit (14:6).

Writers differ on which English word best translates *paraklētos*. The translation "Comforter" was the meaning the Greek fathers ordinarily attached to the word (for example, Origen, Epiphanius, Chrysostom, Cyril of Jerusalem, and Gregory of Nyssa). John Wycliffe (1320–1384) and William Tyndale (1492–1536) were two of the first modern translators to use the rendering "Comforter."

In classical Greek the word is used of a legal advocate or defender of the accused. Demosthenes (384–322 B.C.) used the word *paraklētoi* of personal friends pleading for a judge to decide in favor of their accused friend.[5]

Also Philo, early Jewish philosopher (ca. 13 B.C.– A.D. 45), used the word in several instances in the sense of an advocate or intercessor. Philo wrote about Joseph bestowing righteousness on his brothers who had wronged him and declaring that they needed no one else as "paraklete" or intercessor.[6]

There seems to be little doubt that "Paraclete" should be translated "Advocate" or "Defense" in 1 John 2:1. When a Christian sins, Christ pleads his or her case before God, the heavenly Father. He is the Christian's Intercessor.

But how should "Paraclete" be translated when it refers to the Holy Spirit? Some writers prefer the meaning of legal advocate and explain that the Spirit pleads Christ's cause with the believer.[7] But the statements about the Holy Spirit in John 14–16 do not suggest this view. Such a view does not include the many ministries that Christ said the Paraclete would undertake.[8]

Perhaps no single word can capture all the shades of meaning in the word *paraklētos.* The Holy Spirit, as a *paraklētos,* is a consoler, an encourager, a comforter, a strengthener, a counselor, a teacher, a friend, a helper. Possibly the best rendering of *paraklētos* when it refers to the Holy Spirit is "Helper" (as in the NASB).[9] This seems preferable to the translation "Comforter" for four reasons.

First, the Greek word is a passive form, not an active form. Literally the word means "one who is called alongside" (from *para,* "alongside," and *klētos,* "one called"), not "one who calls alongside of." If this active sense were intended, the word *paraklētor* would be expected. Obviously, then, one who is called to be alongside someone is a "helper."

Second, to speak of the Spirit (as Christ did in John 14:16) as "another Comforter" would imply that Christ too was a Comforter. This limits the concept of who Christ is, for He is far more than a Comforter.

Third, as the word developed in usage, it came to mean "helper in general." A legal advocate who defends is one who helps by counseling, instructing, exhorting, advising, befriending, and attending to the defendant's personal interests.

Fourth, "Helper" designates an inclusive ministry, clearly indicated by the contexts of the passages in which Christ used the term. He said that the Paraclete will show the disciples the things of Christ; teach them things to come; teach them all things; refresh their memories about past teaching; bear witness to Christ; indwell believers; convict of sin, righteousness, and judgment; and be given and sent by the Father to console the disciples in Christ's absence and to continue Christ's work. (However, the thought of advocating and comforting need not be excluded from the meaning of the term. "Helper" here may well embrace the thought of helping by interceding as an advocate and helping by giving comfort. Apparently this explains the NIV's rendering "Counselor.")

The Holy Spirit is "one called alongside" to be the Helper of believers in every situation. He helps as their Defender, their Comforter, their Teacher, their Protector, their Counselor, their Guide, their Exhorter, their Friend. He stands by them and renders any needed assistance.[10] He occupies Himself with the interests, comforts, needs, difficulties, ignorances, trials, and temptations of every child of God.

The fact that the Paraclete is equated three times with the Spirit of truth (John 14:17; 15:26; 16:13) shows that teaching is one aspect of the Paraclete's helping ministry.

As our Paraclete, the Holy Spirit is our Support in weaknesses, our Counselor in difficulties, our Consoler in afflictions, our Teacher in ignorance. [11]

SPIRIT OF WISDOM AND REVELATION

Paul prayed that "the God of our Lord Jesus Christ, the glorious Father, may give you the Spirit of wisdom and revelation" (Eph. 1:17).

Bible students differ on whether the word "spirit" here refers to the human spirit or the Holy Spirit. If the word refers to the human spirit, it should not be capitalized (as in the KJV and the NASB); if it refers to the Holy Spirit then, of course, it should be capitalized (as in the NKJV and the NIV).

Those who suggest that it means man's spirit give this translation: "May the glorious Father give to you a wise spirit and revelation," or "a spirit of wisdom and revelation."[12] But the major objection to this view is that revelation cannot be thought of as a gift given to people for discerning or *understanding* spiritual mysteries. Rather, revelation means a *disclosing* of mysteries. Revelation is the work of God by which He discloses truth to people, not an ability given by God to them for comprehending truth. Thus it would seem strange for Paul to pray that God would give believers revelation. Also, in what sense would believers have an inner attitude ("spirit") of "revelation"?

The more acceptable view of Ephesians 1:17 takes wisdom and revelation as benefits given by the Holy Spirit, not characteristics of the human spirit.[13] Though all believers are indwelt by the Holy Spirit, Paul could pray this prayer in the sense that he wanted the Spirit to minister abundantly to them by giving them these benefits. Paul's prayer was that believers through the Holy Spirit would understand spiritual things and see the "full knowledge" of God. As Albert Barnes put it, "It is probable here that by the word 'spirit' the apostle refers to the Holy Spirit as the Author of all wisdom, and the Revealer of all truth. His prayer is, that God would grant to them the Holy Spirit to make them wise, and to reveal His will to them."[14]

Dickason suggests that this title "speaks of the Spirit's work as 'wising us up' by revelation."[15] He adds: "The work involved here might have once included fresh revelation, as to the Ephesians in a day when Scripture was not yet complete and the gift of prophecy was still needed for the beginning stages of the Church Age. But with the completion of the whole New Testament canon, the Spirit's job is to give us wisdom concerning what has been already revealed. . . . His primary responsibility in teaching centers in the revealed truth of Scripture."[16]

The Holy Spirit's work as a Teacher, Revealer, Guide, and Instructor all confirm His deity and personality. Just the title Paraclete alone suffices to point to the Spirit's personality.

As a Teacher, He makes others wise; gives understanding, counsel, power, knowledge, and the fear of the Lord; communicates and applies God's truth; helps in every learning situation; provides spiritual wisdom; and discloses knowledge regarding God.

GIVE IT SOME THOUGHT

1. What comes to mind when you think of the "Spirit of truth" as a title of the Holy Spirit?

2. When have you sensed the Holy Spirit ministering to you as your "Helper"? How has He helped you in your teaching?

3. Have you ever thanked the Lord for giving you wisdom about spiritual things through "the Spirit of wisdom and revelation"? If not, why not do so now, expressing to the Lord your gratitude for the indwelling, enabling ministry of the third person of the Trinity?

CHAPTER 3
THE TEACHING MINISTRIES
OF THE HOLY SPIRIT

FOR SEVERAL YEARS my wife and I have spent a few weeks in the summer in Estes Park, Colorado. In a small church in nearby Allenspark, we've met a number of people who also come to that area for a few weeks or months each year. They call themselves "summer-comers."

In getting acquainted with some of these dear people, one of the first questions I have asked is, "What work are you in? Or if you are retired, what work did you do?"

Knowing an individual's occupation helps acquaint us with who he or she is. What a person does gives us a clue as to what that individual is like.

It's like that with the Holy Spirit. Knowing that He instructs, reminds, guides, declares, and reveals says to us that He is a divine Teacher. And since we as teachers are to relate to *the* Teacher, we need to know about these functions of His, mentioned in these passages (italics added):

> But the Counselor, the Holy Spirit, whom the Father will send in My name, will *teach* you all things and will *remind* you of every-thing I have said to you. (John 14:26)

> I have much more to say to you, more than you can now bear. But when He, the Spirit of truth, comes, He will *guide* you into all truth. He will not speak on His own; He will speak only what He hears, and He will *tell* you what is yet to come. He will bring glory to

Me by taking from what is Mine and *making it known* to you. All that belongs to the Father is Mine. That is why I said the Spirit will take from what is Mine and *make it known* to you. (16:12–15)

But God has *revealed* it to us by His Spirit. The Spirit searches all things, even the deep things of God. For who among men knows the thoughts of a man except the man's spirit within him? In the same way no one knows the thoughts of God except the Spirit of God. We have not received the spirit of the world but the Spirit who is from God, that we may understand what God has freely given us. This is what we speak, not in words taught us by human wisdom but in words taught by the Spirit, expressing spiritual truths in spiritual words. (1 Cor. 2:10–13)

The promises of divine instruction given in these verses pertain to several areas: (1) instruction in "all things" (John 14:26); (2) recollection of Christ's past utterances (14:26); (3) guidance "into all truth" (16:13); (4) declaration of future events (16:13); and (5) revelation of the "deep things" of God (1 Cor. 2:10).

What does the Spirit teach? Whom does He teach? What does He bring to remembrance? How does He guide? What does He declare? What does He reveal? Examining these verses can help us see how the Holy Spirit specifically conducts His teaching ministry.

THE HOLY SPIRIT INSTRUCTS

The word *didaxei* (from *didaskō*), translated "teach" in John 14:26, carries the meaning of instructing, delivering a discourse, explaining truth. In this verse the verb's indirect object "you" and its direct object "all things" point out the relevant, active nature of imparting truth from one person (the teacher) to other persons (the students). The Holy Spirit's teaching involves content or truth ("all things") and is directed toward individuals ("you"). But to whom does "you" refer? And what is meant by "all things"?

Some interpreters limit the word "you" to the few disciples who were with Christ on earth, without seeking to assign any direct application of the Spirit's teaching to Christians today. But parallel passages indicate otherwise. In the very same chapter (14:17), "the world" is said to be incapable of receiving, beholding, or knowing the Spirit of truth. If the world cannot receive the Spirit and His truths, then the implication is that all those who are *not* of the world, that is, all believers, are capable of receiving His truths. In the same verse Christ's promise that the Spirit "shall be *in you*" clearly refers to all believers, for they are all indwelt by the Spirit of God (Rom. 8:9; 2 Cor. 1:22; 1 John 3:24). The fact that "the man without the Spirit ['the natural man,' KJV] does not accept the things that come from the Spirit of God" (1 Cor. 2:14) indicates that someone other than the unsaved *can* receive them.

However, though all believers are potentially capable of receiving the Spirit's teaching, not all actually do, because the things of God are revealed by the Spirit only *to spiritual* (Spirit-filled) Christians.[1] That there are two classes of Christians, some worldly and others spiritual, is clear from 1 Corinthians 3:1: "*Brothers,* I could not address you as spiritual but as worldly" (italics added).

Only "spiritual" Christians—those who are manifesting the fruit of the Spirit (Gal. 5:22), walking in the Spirit (5:16), and filled with the Spirit (Eph. 5:18)—can receive "the things that come from the Spirit of God . . . because they are spiritually discerned. The spiritual man makes judgments about all things, but he himself is not subject to any man's judgment" (1 Cor. 2:14–15). The word *anakrinei*, translated "makes judgments about," is an Athenian law term meaning "to discern or examine" and refers to a preliminary examination before a judge. Paul's thought, then, is that "the unspiritual are out of court as religious critics."[2] Carnality or worldliness squelches a Christian's spiritual judgment and dulls him to the Holy Spirit's teaching ministry. The "you," then, refers to spiritual Christians, that is, believers in fellowship with Christ.

The words "all things" (John 14:26; 1 Cor. 2:10; 1 John 2:20, 27) and "all truth" (John 16:13) are puzzling because it is difficult to comprehend how the Holy Spirit teaches *every* kind of universal knowledge to spiritual believers. Yet the word "all" is used without reservation. But if the "all things" refers to scientific, universal knowledge, this would mean that Spirit-filled Christians could claim omniscience. This, in turn, would suggest that human teachers are unnecessary.

Many writers see in the words "all things" the fullness of Christian knowledge regarding the plan of salvation.[3] However, there is warrant for expanding the meaning beyond simply salvation or redemption truth to the broader concept of "all that belongs to the sphere of spiritual truth [so that] nothing that is essential to the knowledge of God or the guidance of life shall be wanting."[4] This broader concept is based on parallel phrases found elsewhere in Scripture. The Spirit "will speak only what He hears" (John 16:13), which is explained as "all that belongs to the Father" and the things that are "Mine," that is, Christ's (16:14–15). The "all things" the Spirit searches are not universal knowledge but are "the deep things of God" and "what God has freely given us" (1 Cor. 2:10, 12). These are also the things of which Paul spoke (2:13). Obviously these things do not refer to all areas of life and truth, and yet they are more than salvation truths. They are all truths pertaining to God and His person and work. Knowledge of God and the full body of revealed truth is imparted by the Spirit to those Christians who are spiritually receptive to His teaching. "All the truth" (as the Greek literally reads) is not encyclopedic truth in general but all *revealed* truth, recorded in God's written Word.

A form of the Greek word for "teach" or "instruct," which is used in John 14:26, is also in 1 Corinthians 2:13. The verse reads: "This is what we speak, not in words taught us by human wisdom but in words taught by the Spirit, expressing spiritual truths in spiritual words." The things expressing "we speak" are "what God has freely given us" (2:12), things that believers know because they have received "the Spirit who is from God." These are "the thoughts of God" (2:11), the things God has "prepared for those who love Him" (2:9). Christians speak, then, the revealed things of God "not in human wisdom-taught words, but in [words] Spirit taught" (as the Greek text reads). Paul claimed that the work of the Holy Spirit in revealing truths extends to the words. Spiritual truth *revealed* by the Spirit (2:10) is spoken in spiritual words *taught by* the Spirit (2:13).[5] (This is good support for believing that the inspiration of Scripture extends to words, that inspiration of the Bible is verbal. The phrase "expressing spiritual truths in spiritual words" fits the idea that spiritual concepts in revelation are combined with [*synkrinontes*, "putting, comparing"] spiritual words in inspiration.)

THE HOLY SPIRIT REMINDS

The ministry of reminding is ascribed to the Spirit in only one verse, John 14:26, which also mentions the Spirit's teaching ministry: "But the Counselor, the Holy Spirit, whom the Father will send in My name, will teach you all things, and will remind you of everything I said to you."

After Christ's departure, the Holy Spirit was to stimulate the minds of the disciples to recall the oral teachings and utterances of their Lord. "All this I have spoken," Christ said, "while still with you" (14:25).

This ministry guaranteed the inerrancy of the apostles' inspired writings of the Gospels.[6] But in addition to that, it was a part of the Spirit's teaching ministry to the disciples. "He instructs from within and recalls to the [disciples'] memory what Jesus taught. The Spirit will, therefore, impress the commandments of Jesus on the minds of his disciples."[7]

Many of the things Christ spoke to His disciples had been forgotten by them. And much of what He said was not comprehended at the time, and so would be more easily forgotten (Mark 9:32; John 2:22; 12:16; 20:9). Many of Jesus' utterances were obscure to His disciples because of their insufficient spiritual background. "I have much more to say to you, more than you can now bear" (16:12). They were sorrowful and confused about His coming departure (Luke 18:34; John 13:33–37; 14:1–5) and concerned about a traitor among them (13:21–25). These facts may have made them insensitive to more spiritual truth.

Obviously believers today are not reminded of Christ's oral sayings as such, because they did not hear them. But the Holy Spirit does remind Christians of Christ's *recorded* sayings in the Gospels. And, of course, the teaching of the Spirit goes beyond just those recorded sayings of Christ.

The Spirit of truth guides into all the truth (John 16:13)—all the written Word of God.

THE HOLY SPIRIT GUIDES

In John 16:13 the Greek word translated "will guide" is *hodēgēsei.* It is from *hodēgeō,* a combination of *hodos,* "way or road," and *agō,* "to lead."

Thus it literally means "lead the way" or "guide along the way or road." It reflects a Guide who leads travelers into unknown territory. A guide directs or leads others into paths previously unfamiliar to them. This is the thought brought out in the previous verse (16:12). The disciples were unfamiliar with some truth; they needed the Holy Spirit to lead them into it. As a Guide, the Spirit points the way (hodos) to the truth, and Christ is both the way and the truth (14:6).

Coming to know or understand truth is frequently depicted in Scripture as taking place with the help of a guide. Teaching is thought of as "leading the way." The Ethiopian eunuch asked, "How can I [understand what I read], except some man should guide [hodēgēsei] me?" (Acts 8:31, KJV) Guidance (help in understanding) was needed so he could comprehend the truth of what he read. And David asked that God would "guide" (hodēgēson in the Septuagint) him "in Your truth" and that the Lord would teach him (Ps. 25:5). David also prayed that the Holy Spirit would "lead" (hodēgēsei) him along a level path (143:10).

Since Jesus was addressing the twelve disciples in John 16:12–13, His promise that the Spirit of truth would guide them "into all truth" was directed to them. The Twelve would come to understand "the specific truth about the person of Jesus and the significance of what He said and did."[8]

The Holy Spirit, Christ promised, would guide—not drive or compel—the disciples "into all truth." The order of the Greek words emphasizes the adjective "all" and implies two things: (1) the Holy Spirit did not stress one truth at the expense of all others, and (2) the Spirit guided into all truth, whereas Christ revealed only a portion of what He would like to have unfolded. To the disciples the Spirit clarified and amplified what Christ had given in germ form, and the Spirit unfolded what Christ had withheld. Much of what Jesus had said was not understood by the disciples (Mark 9:32; Luke 9:45; John 8:27; 10:6; 12:16). But after Jesus was glorified (ascended, 12:16) and the Holy Spirit came on the Day of Pentecost to indwell believers, the apostles then understood the significance of Jesus' words regarding Himself and His death and resurrection.

Some Bible commentators believe the guidance of the Spirit in John 16:13 refers to the Spirit's work of inspiration, leading the disciples in writing New Testament books.[9] However, the word "guide" speaks more of instructing than of inspiring (see Acts 8:31; Pss. 25:5; 143:10), of helping to understand rather than helping to record. In addition, it seems unlikely that Christ was addressing the disciples about writing inspired Scripture because only three of the Twelve (Matthew, John, and Peter) wrote New Testament books.

After Pentecost the disciples were led to a greater comprehension of the person and work of Jesus Christ. As a result, they were changed men, individuals filled with the Holy Spirit and His power. Though John 16:13 was addressed specifically to the Twelve, all believers may be similarly guided into the truth about Christ (led along the path of truth). As Christ had said earlier, those who are His disciples would "know the truth" (8:31–32).

The Holy Spirit does not unfold new revelations beyond the boundaries of Christ's teachings or the Bible. This is clear from the statement in John 16:13 where Jesus told His disciples "He [the Spirit] will not speak on His own, He will speak only what He hears." He shows those things that He has received from Christ (16:15).

This does not mean, as some suppose, that the Spirit does not speak about Himself. Rather, He does not speak *from* Himself, independently of the Father and the Son. The Father, the Son, and the Spirit are one in essence. Therefore what the Spirit hears from the Father (16:13) and takes from the Son (16:15), He communicates to believers.

What the Spirit hears is obviously in keeping with what Christ desired to teach the disciples. As He guides, the Holy Spirit enlarges on what Christ taught, without teaching independently of the Father and the Son. Not speaking from Himself, He then guided the disciples and now guides believers into what He hears and receives, namely, all the truth, all the revelation of God.

But are all believers automatically led by the Spirit into all the truth? Obviously not, for guidance implies obedience to the Guide and a willingness to be led. We believers advance and grow in the grace and knowledge of the Lord Jesus Christ (2 Pet. 3:18) only as we are willing to be guided by the Holy Spirit, our divine Teacher.

THE HOLY SPIRIT DECLARES

Declaring or announcing things to come is another phase of the teaching work of the Holy Spirit. In John 16:13–15 the Greek verb *anangelei* occurs three times: "He will tell [*anangelei*] you what is yet to come"; "He will bring glory by taking from what is Mine and making it known [*anangelai*] to you"; "the Spirit will take from what is Mine and make it known [*anangelei*] to you." The KJV translates *anangelai* "declare" and the NASB translates it "disclose." The same word is also used in John 4:25 ("explain"), 16:25 ("tell plainly"), 1 Peter 1:12 ("told"), and 1 John 1:5 ("declare").

What is meant by "the things that are coming" (the Greek has the present tense)? Some writers suggest that the verse is a promise to the disciples that under the Spirit's inspiration they would write New Testament books dealing with future events.[10] But if this were the case, "tell," "announce," or "declare" is hardly the verb to be expected. Just as recollection of Christ's oral utterances is not to be identified with the inspiration of the Gospels, so the announcement of things that are coming is not to be identified with the inspiration of the Epistles and the Apocalypse.

Also, it is unlikely that this refers to the gift of prophecy, as Lindars suggests.[11]

Several expositors assume that "the things that are coming" refers to prophecies of future events at the time of Christ's return. Many others suggest the words meant to *the disciples* the things that were soon to come in the new church age in the near *as well as* the not-so-near future rather than *exclusively* the last days at the time of Christ's second coming.[12] Tasker emphasizes the near future from the disciples' perspective. "The things that are coming," he suggests, refers to Jesus' death and resurrection, which He spoke of in the Upper Room Discourse and about which the apostles were illuminated by the Spirit after Pentecost.[13]

Though addressed specifically to the Twelve, the promise of the Spirit's disclosing things to come may apply to believers today. He does this by illuminating their minds and hearts regarding what God has already revealed in His Word about His program for the world and present-day Christian living. These are the things, Christ said, that are "Mine." What to Christ's disciples were "things that are coming" are to believers today "things that are present," that is, all that is revealed in the New Testament about God's workings in this present age. The Holy Spirit teaches believers these things from His holy Word. This is a major part of His teaching ministry.

THE HOLY SPIRIT REVEALS

The truth of God, unknown by people who have not experienced God's salvation, is revealed by the Holy Spirit to those who love the Lord. As Paul stated, "However, as it is written: 'No eye has seen, no ear has heard, no mind has conceived what God has prepared for those who love Him' but God has revealed it to us by His Spirit" (1 Cor. 2:9–10).

Walvoord makes this pointed observation about this passage: "Here is an epistemology that transcends the human senses. God is known by a process that does not involve the eye or the ear, nor does it originate in the heart, or human consciousness. Here is a frontal denial of empiricism, the idea that all knowledge comes through the senses. Knowledge comes through the ministry of the Holy Spirit of God."[14]

The Holy Spirit is the instrument through whom God reveals to Christians "what God has prepared" (2:9), "the deep things of God"[15] which "the Spirit searches" (2:10), "what God has freely given us" (2:12), and "the things that come from the Spirit of God"(2:14).

Because the Holy Spirit, the third person of the Trinity, comprehends the depths of God's nature, He is competent to reveal the things of God to humans. The verses that follow in 1 Corinthians 2 expound this fact in further detail by the analogy of a person's spirit and God's Spirit. As only a person's inner spirit knows his thoughts, so only the Spirit of God truly knows God and His thoughts (2:11).

But if only the Holy Spirit knows God, how can *human beings* know God? The answer is, by the Spirit of God whom believers have received (2:12). He reveals God and His truths to "those who love Him" (2:9).

No one can know the plans, thoughts, and intentions of another person unless that person chooses to reveal them. So it is with God. No one can know His plans and designs unless He chooses to make them known by His Spirit. And He has chosen to do this. Having received the Spirit of God at salvation, Christians may know, as the Spirit teaches them, "the things . . . of God" (2:12, KJV).

The word for "know" in 1 Corinthians 2:12 suggests that, because of the teaching work of the indwelling Holy Spirit, believers possess an inherent knowledge of the things of God revealed in His Word—things that eye, ear, and heart are unable to know or comprehend through seeing, hearing, or feeling. How privileged are Christians to know through God's Spirit and God's Word something of the very heart, nature, and plans of God!

MAKE IT PERSONAL

1. Would you consider yourself a "spiritual" Christian, that is, one who is filled with the Holy Spirit? Or is some sin in your life hindering the Holy Spirit manifesting His "fruit" in you?
2. Are you obeying the Lord and His Word so that the Holy Spirit can guide you into an understanding of divine truth?
3. Have you recently thanked God for the unique privilege of knowing through the Holy Spirit something of God's nature and plans? If not, why not express thanks to Him now?

CHAPTER 4
MINISTRIES OF THE SPIRIT
RELATED TO TEACHING

SEVERAL OTHER MINISTRIES of the Spirit are closely related to His works of teaching. They are inspiration, conviction, indwelling, and illumination. (The Holy Spirit's relationship to interpretation, an aspect of illumination, is discussed in chapter 10.)

INSPIRATION AND TEACHING

Inspiration is that supernatural work of the Holy Spirit whereby He so guided and superintended the writers of Scripture that what they wrote is the Word of God, inerrant as originally written (2 Pet. 1:21). The personalities and styles of the writers were not obliterated by this action of the Holy Spirit. This "breathing" of God (2 Tim. 3:16) into the writings was an act both verbal (the Spirit guided in the choice of the words—which cannot be separated from thoughts)—and plenary (inspiration extended to every portion of the Bible so that it is infallible in truth and final in authority). The Greek word for "inspired" (2 Tim. 3:16, NASB) is *theopneustos,* literally, "God-breathed" (as the NIV translates it). Because of its divine origin and nature, the Bible in its original manuscripts was without error. True, God used human authors to record His truth, but He is capable of protecting them from error. If the Bible's original manuscripts contained even a few mistakes, how can we say that any of it is reliable? Since God is true (1 Thess. 1:9; 1 John 5:20) and cannot lie (Titus 1:2; Heb. 6:18), He can and did preserve His Word from error.[1]

Inspiration differs from teaching in the following ways:

First, only the writers of Scripture were involved in the Spirit's work of inspiration, whereas *all* believers may receive the Spirit's teaching.

Second Peter 1:21 states the method the Spirit used in the act of inspiration. The writers were "carried along" by the Spirit, much as a sailboat is borne along by the wind. The Bible never suggests that anyone other than those holy men of God who were superintended to pen the words of Scripture are "carried along" by the Spirit. The fact that the canon of Scripture is closed indicates that the Spirit is no longer speaking through human authors to inspire new Scripture. As discussed in chapter 3, Christ was addressing *all* believers, not just the disciples, when He stated in John 14:26 and 16:13 that He "will teach *you* all things" and "He will guide *you* into all truth" (italics added). Certainly, while no mature Christian would claim to be guided by the Spirit of God to write biblical revelation beyond the limits of the scriptural canon, many believers can attest that God's Spirit has guided them into understanding and appropriating revealed truth, "the faith that was once for all entrusted to the saints" (Jude 3).

Second, inspiration was an act once for all completed when the Spirit composed the sixty-sixth book of the Bible. The Holy Spirit no longer has a ministry of inspiration; that act is past, and the canon is complete. On the other hand, the Holy Spirit is presently engaged in a continuous ministry of instruction. The departure of Christ into heaven enabled the Spirit to come and minister in His stead (John 14:16–19, 26; 16:7,13, 16). The fact that Christ is still positioned in heaven clearly indicates that the Holy Spirit carries on in Christ's absence as His "substitute Teacher."

Third, inspiration is the act of God the Spirit in which He caused writers *to record* God's revelation. Thus, in a sense, inspiration is revelation, an unveiling. However, to be precise, in inspiration the human authors were used of God to seal in writing the truth that God at the time was unveiling about Himself in words. The Bible is revelation (not only a record of revelation), and inspiration was the act whereby God put the revealed truths into infallible written form. Revelation is the communication of truth that would not otherwise be known, whereas inspiration is the process whereby this information is presented accurately in written language. Revelation is

32

the Spirit's disclosure of divine truth, whereas inspiration is the Spirit's superintending process of recording His revelation.

In Scripture the two sometimes converge. This explains why they are sometimes confused. Revelation sometimes occurred without inspiration, as illustrated in Exodus 20:22 (where the Lord said to Moses, "Tell the Israelites this: 'You have seen yourselves that I have spoken to you from heaven'") and Revelation 10:4 ("I heard a voice from heaven say, 'Seal up what the seven thunders have said and do not write it down'"). And inspiration sometimes did not involve revealing of new, previously undisclosed truth, as seen in 1 Timothy 5:18 ("For the Scripture says, 'Do not muzzle the ox while it is treading out the grain,' and 'The worker deserves his wages'").

Distinct from inspiration, divine teaching is the work of the Spirit enabling believers to understand and personally appropriate this recorded revelation. As J. I. Packer explains, "And 'he that is spiritual'—he in whom the Spirit abides to give understanding—discerns the meaning of the message and receives it as the testimony of God."[2]

Fourth, though borne along by the Spirit, the human authors of the Bible did not always understand what they wrote. This is particularly noted in 1 Peter 1:10–11: "Concerning this salvation, the prophets, who spoke of the grace that was to come to you, searched intently and with the greatest care, trying to find out the time and circumstances to which the Spirit of Christ in them was pointing when He predicted the sufferings of Christ and the glories that would follow."

The authors' lack of understanding of what they wrote in no way detracted from the certainty of their being divinely used in inspiration.

In contrast to this is the fact that the Spirit's purpose in teaching is to make clear to the minds and hearts of God's children the truth He has inspired.

If the Spirit's inspiring ministry is equated with His teaching ministry, inspiration tends to be degraded to a universally available mystical influence or provision of spiritual insight. This makes the human authors of Scripture differ from other Christians only in that "they were pioneers of conscience, and the consciousness of a divine commission made them prophets."[3] This is the view of Friedrich Schleiermacher (1768–1834), who taught that the writers of Scripture were awakened in their religious consciousness and given religious intuitive feelings and insights. To confuse inspiration with the teaching of the Spirit debases Scripture or elevates the words of believers to the level of the Scriptures. L. Gaussen illustrates how Jewish scholasticism and Roman Catholicism have been guilty of the latter.[4]

CONVICTION AND TEACHING

The ascension of Christ made possible the descent of the Spirit to "convict the world in regard to sin and righteousness and judgment" (John 16:8). This verse precedes the statement that the Spirit, "when He . . . comes," will guide believers "into all truth" (16:13). Thus His coming provided for His carrying on two ministries: convicting the world and teaching believers. But what does the former of these mean? And how does it relate to His teaching of believers?

The word *elenchei* (from *elenchō,* "convict") implies demonstrating by argument, refuting by proofs, *convincing* by means of unanswerable arguments.[5] The Greek courts of justice used the word in a legal sense to mean "convince of guilt."[6] It was not primarily the reprimand of the guilty one but rather the logical unanswerable demonstration of the *fact* of his guilt, thereby making him conscious of his guilt. Thus the word did not convey so much the thought of bringing one to the point of *sorrow* for his sin as it did the idea of demonstrating the *guilt* of his sin.

This meaning is illustrated by the words of Christ in John 8:46: "Can any of you prove Me guilty *(elenchei)* of sin?" He did not mean, "Which of you can make Me feel sorry for sin?" Instead, He was asking, "Which of you can find proof that I am guilty?"

Sorrow of heart and, in turn, salvation may or may not follow from the convincing work of the Spirit. As the Holy Spirit *convinces* sinners regarding sin, righteousness, and judgment (16:8–11), some of them acknowledge their guilt, are sorrowful for sin, and turn to God for salvation, while others reject Christ.

In this ministry of convincing or demonstrating the guilt of sin, the Holy Spirit is, in a sense, "teaching" the unsaved. They are brought in contact with certain truths. They are "enlightened" regarding their sin, the need of righteousness through Christ, and the judgment of sin. The Spirit places the truth in a clear light before sinners so that it may be seen and acknowledged as truth. John Calvin called this ministry the Holy Spirit's "inner witness" or "internal testimony." "It is His work whereby He witnesses to and convinces a person at the moment of salvation regarding the certainty of the truth of Scripture."[7] As stated by the International Council on Biblical Inerrancy, "The Holy Spirit, Scripture's divine author, both authenticates it to us by His inward witness and opens our minds to understand its meaning."[8]

Some, like Calvin, refer to this convincing work as an illuminating or enlightening of the unsaved, separate from the illuminating of the saved. Many consider it an "instructing" aspect of the work of the Spirit in common grace,[9] bestowed on every unregenerate person. This is referred to in John 1:9, "The true light that gives light to *every man* was coming into the world" (italics added). Unbelievers are enlightened (or taught by demonstrable proof) concerning their sin, God's righteousness, and the work of the Cross. The enlightenment may come through the preaching of the Word of God or by the direct, personal work of the Spirit on the mind and heart through the Word of God. In this enlightening, the Spirit is operating as Teacher, because He is illuminating certain truths necessary for salvation by faith in Jesus Christ.

Chafer summarizes this truth in this way: "When the Spirit enlightens the Satan-blinded mind regarding sin, righteousness, and judgment, that otherwise blinded mind is at once more than normally enabled to understand the three great foundational truths that sin has been judged, righteousness is available in and through Christ, and the condemning sin is failure to believe that which God now offers the sinner, namely, a perfect salvation in and through Christ the Saviour. No soul can be saved apart from this enlightenment, for no other power is sufficient to break the blindness which Satan has imposed on the minds of those who are lost."[10]

INDWELLING AND TEACHING

While the Spirit's indwelling of believers is not a teaching ministry as such, it is the basis for His teaching. Two verses in 1 John reveal the close relationship between the Spirit's indwelling and His teaching: "But you have an anointing from the Holy One, and all of you know the truth" (1 John 2:20). "As for you, the anointing you received from Him remains in you, and you do not need anyone to teach you. But as His anointing teaches you about all things and as that anointing is real, not counterfeit—just as it has taught you, remain in Him" (2:27).

Though the Holy Spirit is not explicitly referred to in these verses, He is certainly implied, as several factors indicate. First, the figure of oil, which often symbolizes the Holy Spirit (Pss. 45:7; 105:15; Isa. 61:1; Acts 10:38), is used. Second, "the anointing" refers to the Holy Spirit, because the anointing comes from "the Holy One," who is Christ, according to Mark 1:24; John 6:69; Acts 3:14; 4:27, 30; and Revelation 3:7. Christ promised to send the Spirit (John 14:26; 15:26; 16:7, 14). Third, 2 Corinthians 1:21–22, parallel to the passages in 1 John, clearly refers to the Holy Spirit. Fourth, the "anointing" is said in 1 John 2:27 to indwell believers ("remains in you"), and this is a work of the Spirit frequently referred to in the Scriptures (Rom. 8:9,11; 1 Cor. 3:16; 6:19; Eph. 2:22; 2 Tim. 1:14; 1 John 3:24). Fifth, the fact that 1 John 2:27 states the anointing "teaches" suggests that the anointing refers to the Holy Spirit. Sixth, Jesus was anointed by the Holy Spirit (Acts 10:38). The Spirit is called "the anointing" because the act (anointing) represents the effect (imparting of the Spirit).

This anointing or indwelling of the Spirit is a once-for-all act that occurs at the moment of salvation. It is a permanent—not temporary—experience ("the anointing . . . remains in you," 1 John 2:27) that makes it possible for Christians to be taught God's truth ("His anointing teaches you"). This does not mean, however, that every believer is necessarily fully taught by the Spirit. "While the anointing with the Spirit makes possible His teaching ministry to the saint, it does not determine the fullness, richness, efficiency, or extent of that ministry. Every saint is anointed with the Spirit. But every saint is not the recipient of the best services of the Spirit in His teaching ministry."[11]

Perhaps the greatest problem in these two verses is the seeming exclusion of the need for human teachers, as indicated in the words "and you know all things" (1 John 2:20, NIV marg.; NKJV) and "you do not need anyone to teach you" (2:27). Do these verses mean that when the Holy

Spirit indwells believers, He no longer uses human channels to impart His truth, and that believers have no need for further instruction because they possess all knowledge?

At least three interpretations have been given to the clause in 1 John 2:20. One involves making the verse read, as in the NIV, "all [*pantes,* masculine nominative plural] of you know," rather than, "you know all things [*panta,* neuter accusative plural]." Since strong Greek manuscript evidence favors each reading, it is difficult to decide the issue on textual evidence alone. In favor of *pantes* ("all of you"), as Bruce points out, is the fact that it is the more difficult reading and therefore was more likely to have been changed by scribal copyists than vice versa.[12] If *pantes* is the preferred reading, then John was saying that all his readers (true believers) have knowledge of Christ (Eph. 4:21; Col. 1:28) in contrast to the false teachers' claim that only *they* had scriptural insight (1 John 4:1).

On the other hand, in favor of *panta* ("all things") as the original reading is the possibility that *panta* may have been mistakenly influenced by *pantes* in 1 John 2:19, "they *all* are not of us" (NASB). Also since the Greek verb *oida* ("know") always has an object, it would seem strange for John to say "you all know." (The NIV supplies the words "the truth" as the object of *oida,* but those words are not in the Greek text.) "You know all things" also is more consistent with 1 John 2:27, "His anointing teaches you about [*peri*] all things [*panton,* neuter genitive plural]." Another interpretation supplies the word *needful* to the thought of the verse: "And you know all needful things," that is, all things necessary for Christian living. But this seems to be inserting a thought not originally intended by the Holy Spirit.

A third view takes the verse as it reads in the NIV margin, "and you know all things," and understands it to mean the same thing John meant when he wrote, "the Holy Spirit . . . will teach you all things" (John 14:26), "He shall guide you into all truth" (16:13), and "His anointing teaches you about all things" (1 John 2:27). The meaning then, as Plummer put it, is, "It is you (and not these antichristian Gnostics who claim it) that are in possession of the true knowledge, in virtue of the anointing of the Spirit of truth."[13] Gnostics in the early church claimed to know God's truth but actually did not. They even claimed to be anointed and thus to be above all others spiritually. But all true believers, John wrote, know all God's truth without having to rely on the Gnostics, because only believers are truly anointed by the Holy Spirit. Westcott explains that because believers have the gift of the Holy Spirit they "have potentially complete and certain knowledge: no false teaching can deceive" them.[14] They do not need to add to their knowledge the teachings of the Gnostics. Nor are Christians limited to some gnostic-like hobbyhorse doctrine to the neglect of "all the counsel of God" (Acts 20:27, KJV).

In 1 John 2:27 the clause "And you do not need anyone to teach you" also needs careful consideration. The word "teach" is in the present tense, emphasizing continuous action. A literal translation would be, "And you have no need that anyone be teaching you."

This clause, too, has been explained in various ways. Kuyper takes it to mean that the church as a body needs no "outsider" to teach it, because it possesses all the treasures of wisdom and knowledge in Christ, its Head.[15] This is also the view of Bruce: "They [do not] need any one from outside . . . to teach them. It is within the fellowship that the Spirit operates; it is there that He teaches the people of God."[16]

A second view is that John is saying, "You need not be taught, only reminded" (in accord with the statement in John 14:26). Robertson holds this view.[17]

A third explanation refers it to repetition in teaching. Lenski paraphrases, "You are not a group of ignoramuses that need to be taught over and over by apostles and by Christian teachers."[18]

Alford presents a fourth view: They have no need of any teaching at all.[19]

A fifth and perhaps the best view understands the problem as one of ultimate or exclusive source or authority. Wuest succinctly explains: "It merely means that the saints are not at the mercy of these Gnostic teachers or at the mercy of any teachers, for that matter. No teacher, even a God-appointed one, is the only and ultimate source of the saint's instruction. He has the Holy Spirit and the Word."[20]

This is similar to the interpretation suggested earlier for verse 20. Marshall holds this view, stating that the last part of verse 27 "is an exhortation to hold fast to the teaching given by the Spirit rather than to be tempted by the false teachers."[21] Because Christians have the indwelling Holy Spirit, they can test the teachings people present to them. And the apostle John added, "That anointing is real, not counterfeit." The false teachers claimed to have an anointing, a special form of inspiration, but it was false. A. B. Simpson explains it this way: "It does not mean that we are not to receive the message of God from human lips; but it does mean we are not to receive any messages as the word of man, but, even when we are taught by the ministers of Christ, we are to receive them as the messengers of God, to compare their word with God's Holy Word, and only to receive it as it is the voice of God speaking to our conscience in the Holy Ghost."[22]

Though God uses Christian teachers to communicate His Word, ultimately learners are taught by God (John 6:45a; 14:26; 16:13). The believers whom John was addressing especially needed this thought emphasized. They were in danger of following the man-made teachings of Gnosticism rather than seeking to continue to be taught by the Holy Spirit through the Word.[23] Donald Burdick puts it this way: "What the indwelling Spirit had already taught them was perfectly adequate. It could not be superseded.... The apostle was magnifying the ability of Christian laypersons to understand spiritual truth with the aid of the Holy Spirit."[24]

Whatever the verse means, it clearly does *not* mean that the Spirit supersedes all need for human instruction. First John 2:1, 24 indicate that even John himself was teaching his readers through his epistle!

The second half of 1 John 2:27 ought not be overlooked: "But as His anointing teaches you about all things and as that anointing is real, not counterfeit—just as it has taught you, remain [or, abide] in Him." "Anointing" represents the effect of the act of anointing, namely, the Holy Spirit who comes at salvation to indwell believers. As already discussed, He teaches Christians all things. And since He is the Spirit of truth (John 15:26; 16:13), the anointing is not counterfeit like that of the Gnostics. And because of that true teaching, Christians should abide in Him (remain in fellowship with Christ) to be taught by Him.

Though indwelt by the blessed Holy Spirit, Christians are capable of receiving the teaching ministry of the Spirit only as they "abide in Him."

ILLUMINATION AND TEACHING

The illuminating work of the Holy Spirit is frequently referred to in Scripture. The Greek word for "enlighten" *(phōtizō)* means "to give light, shine"; "to . . . light up, illumine"; and "to enlighten spiritually, imbue with saving knowledge."[25] The third classification relates this work of the Spirit to that of teaching or bestowing knowledge. The figure is that of the light of knowledge penetrating and dispelling the darkness of ignorance. The following verses show how illumination is related to knowledge:

> For God, who said, "Let light shine out of darkness," made His light shine in our hearts to give us the light [*phōtisuon*] of the knowledge of the glory of God in the face of Christ. (2 Cor. 4:6)

> I keep asking that the God of our Lord Jesus Christ, the glorious Father, may give you the Spirit of wisdom and revelation, so that you may know Him better. I pray also that the eyes of your heart may be enlightened [*pephoutismenous*] in order that you may know the hope to which He has called you, the riches of His glorious inheritance in the saints, and His incomparably great power for us who believe. (Eph. 1:17–19)

Unbelievers are spoken of as being "darkened in their understanding" (4:18). This emphasizes the need for illumination. God has given general and special revelation, but sin has blinded people to it. Thus they cannot receive God's external, objective revelation. God's Word is not in any way defective or insufficient. The fault lies with people. It is as though a blind person were facing the sun. The fact that he cannot see the light is not the sun's fault; the deficiency lies with him.

Non-Christians are spiritually blind. Their hearts are hardened; they are insensitive to God; they are blinded to God's truth. The Holy Spirit must open the eyes of their minds and hearts and give them spiritual enlightenment or illumination. As Calvin wrote, "The Word of God is like the sun shining on all to whom it is preached; but without any benefit to the blind. But in this respect we are all blind by nature, therefore it cannot penetrate into our minds, unless this internal teacher, the Spirit, makes way for it by His illumination."[26]

In one sense all non-Christians are illuminated (John 1:9). But not all are the "sons of light" (12:36). The special work of God's Spirit by which He moves non-Christians to believe the revealed truth of salvation and accept Christ as their Savior is regeneration. In salvation the Holy Spirit convinces a person of the truth of Scripture, opens his mind to understand it and his heart to receive it (illumines), and gives new life (regenerates). New revelation is not given; rather, the person becomes a child of God and therefore receives the capacity to comprehend and appropriate God's revelation, the Bible.

However, saints, too, are in need of illumination, as evidenced by the psalmist's request, "Open my eyes that I may see wonderful things in your law" (Ps. 119:18). Paul prayed that the Ephesian believers would have the eyes of their heart "enlightened" (Eph. 1:18). As Christ talked with the disciples following His resurrection, "He opened their minds so they could understand the Scriptures" (Luke 24:45).

These facts show that illumination is clearly that supernatural work of the Spirit whereby He enables individuals to apprehend the already revealed truth of God. But is this a work of the Spirit on the mind only? Does illumination imply that some believers are able to penetrate Scripture to grasp new truths or "deep" meanings that others cannot understand? Does it imply that new mental faculties are given by the Spirit to some believers, so that they can see underlying truths not readily ascertainable from the text? Does illumination mean that the Holy Spirit gives sudden flashes of insight into the meaning of Scripture? Does this eliminate the need for Bible study?

In answer to these questions five points may be suggested.

First, the Spirit's illumination always relates to the Word of God, the Bible. This is clear from Psalm 119:18, 130; John 14:26; and Revelation 22:18. Illumination, because it is related to the Bible, is not some form of "inner light" or "inner voice" apart from the Word. No new truth is revealed in illumination. The Bible is God's complete written revelation, beyond which the Spirit of God reveals no new truths. To give new truths to non-Christians would be as useless as trying to make a blind man see by putting two suns in the sky.[27] He does not need added content or knowledge; he needs the eyes of his heart opened so he can see the revelation already given.

Second, illumination is more appropriately defined as the work of the Spirit on the mind, enabling a person to understand the truth of God already revealed. (It is wrong to speak of the Holy Spirit illuminating the Scriptures. They do not need light; humans need light.) Ephesians 1:18 speaks of the "eyes of your *heart*" (italics added) being enlightened (the KJV translates "heart" as "understanding"). Lydia's *heart* was opened (Acts 16:14). The mind and heart together comprise what Kuyper calls the "spiritual consciousness."[28] Fred Klooster calls it "heart-understanding."[29] Spiritual truths demand the response of the affections and the will, as well as the understanding.

Third, illumination involves not simply the perception but also the *reception* of truth. It is not so much a mental apprehension of "deep" truths as it is a personal welcome and *appropriation* of truths understood. To receive God's truths fully, one must first understand them and then appropriate them. Geoffrey Bromiley expresses this fact when he says that the Holy Spirit, who has given the Word of God, seeks to "open the eyes of the readers to *perceive* its truth and *receive* its light."[30] As Klooster says: "Understanding Scripture requires more than an intellectual grasp of the historical setting of the text or the literary structure of the passage. . . . Heart-understanding demands the heart response in the totality of one's being to the living, Triune God."[31]

Obviously unsaved people can mentally grasp something of the Bible's objective data. Many unbelievers have understood many of the historical facts presented in the Word of God. Some have even followed biblical logic. They have cognitively grasped certain objective biblical facts—that certain Bible personalities performed certain tasks, said certain words, went to certain geographical locations, argued with certain points of logic, and so on—yet they do not know the God of the Scriptures. "The world through its wisdom did not know Him" (1 Cor. 1:21). Even with determined and diligent research on a high scholarly level, they are unable to respond to the true divine sense of the Scriptures.[32] The Spirit's illumination of Christians, then, must include something more than that mental apprehension of the Bible of which non-Christians are capable.

Though the unsaved may mentally observe objective biblical data, it remains foolishness to them (1 Cor. 1:18; 2:14). Though unbelievers are able to follow the logic of Paul's reasoning in his epistles, they do not "take to heart" the truth involved. The grammar of John 3:16 may be clear to the unsaved, but this does not mean their hearts receive the truth of the verse. The unsaved do not welcome God's truth, because it strikes at the very core of their sinfulness.

Only believers are able to *welcome* God's truth. When Paul stated in 1 Corinthians 2:14 that "the man without the Spirit [*psychikos anthrōpos,* 'soulish, unsaved man'] does not accept the things that come from the Spirit of God," he did not mean that an unsaved person is totally incapable of comprehending any of the Bible's grammatical data. Rather, Paul meant that a non-Christian does not welcome its truth! The Greek word translated "accept" *(dechomai)* means "welcome." If "receive" were intended, a different Greek word *(lambanō)* would have been used. The verse does not mean that an unsaved person, who is devoid of the Holy Spirit, cannot *understand* mentally what the Bible is saying; instead it means that he does not *welcome* its message of redemption to his own heart.[33] He rejects the message, refusing to appropriate it and act on it. By contrast, people in Berea "received [from *dechomai*] the Word with great eagerness" (Acts 17:11, NASB), and the Thessalonians "welcomed [from *dechomai*] the message with the joy given by the Holy Spirit"(1 Thess. 1:6).

The statement in 1 Corinthians 2:14 that the things of the Spirit of God "are foolishness" to an unbeliever would indicate that he has *some* understanding of what the Bible says. Otherwise, if nothing were communicated to him, how could he judge such communication foolish? He could not call something foolishness unless he had some cognitive awareness of it.

"But," someone may argue, "this verse also states that an unsaved person cannot even *know* the things of the Spirit. Doesn't this argue *against* the point being made that the unsaved can be cognizant of Bible facts?" No, because the Greek word that is used means "know by experience" *(ginōskō),* as opposed to the word *oida,* which means "know intuitively or intrinsically." An unbeliever does not know God's truth experientially. He may grasp portions of it mentally, but he does not discern it spiritually nor experience it personally. Virkler summarizes this point this way: "Thus unbelievers do not *know* the full meaning of scriptural teaching, not because that meaning is unavailable to them in the words of the text, but because they refuse to act on and appropriate spiritual truths for their own lives. Furthermore, the psychological results of such refusal make them less and less able (and willing) to comprehend these truths."[34]

Illumination is the Spirit's work, enabling Christians to discern the meaning of the message and to welcome and receive it as from God.

Hodge states that obedience in the believer's life is the inevitable result of the illuminating work of the Spirit.[35]

This concept of illumination is also verified by Christ's words to the unbelieving Pharisees. He did not denounce them for not understanding the facts of the truth; they understood the "letter of the Law" better than perhaps any other people in their day. He denounced them, however, for not appropriating the truth as God's truth. Paul did not rebuke the carnal Corinthians for failing to have a mental grasp of spiritual facts, but for not receiving in their hearts what they understood in their minds. For this reason, he said, "You were not yet ready for it. Indeed, you are still not ready. You are still worldly" (1 Cor. 3:2–3). In illumination the Spirit helps believers understand the implications and values of God's truth and welcome it with a view to personal heartfelt appropriation. "Illumination drives home in the heart what the mind grasps."[36] Illumination gives the believer a taste for God and His truth, a desire for spiritual things, a sense of the beauty of God's truth.

Fourth, illumination is possible only as a believer is open to the Spirit's sanctifying and cleansing work (see chapter 7). Unsaved people do not welcome the truth (2:14); conversely, believers, to receive God's truth, must be open to it. Sin in a Christian's life blocks spiritual maturity and keeps him from being able to appropriate God's Word (3:1–3). One who is not mature spiritually "is not accustomed to the Word of righteousness" (Heb. 5:13, NASB); so he is able to assimilate only "milk and not solid food"(5:12, NASB).

Believers whose hearts are open to the Spirit's enlightenment then "know" (*oida,* "know inherently") God's spiritual "riches." "He who is spiritual appraises [*anakrinetai,* 'discerns'] all things" (1 Cor. 2:15, NASB).

Because the Bible is more than a human book, it can be rightly understood only by those who are divinely enabled by the Holy Spirit. Karl Barth wrongly equated this ministry of the Spirit with His ministry of revelation. J. Theodore Mueller writes that "Barth regards only that as the Word of God which the Spirit impresses upon the individual human mind as such, or as we may say, the Bible is God's Word only so far as God spoke through it. If God does not speak through the Scriptures, they are not God's Word but merely men's word."[37] Barth's view denies the objectivity of divine truth and rejects the infallible authority of the Scriptures. (This will be discussed more fully in chapters 8 and 9.) Without this ministry of the Spirit, the Bible remains a spiritual enigma.

Fifth, illumination occurs in conjunction with and not apart from a believer's diligent study and devoted prayer. The Holy Spirit's illuminating ministry demands study; it does not delete it. One should not think of the Spirit's work as an excuse for laziness, a way to avoid hard work in the study of the Scriptures. Discerning the meaning of a Scripture passage may come suddenly, but it usually results from intense and even prolonged research and pondering. Just as Ezra "devoted himself to [literally, 'set his heart on'] the study" of God's Word (Ezra 7:10), so believers today should eagerly and diligently give themselves to God's Word. As they do, they are more apt to discern its meaning (by the Holy Spirit's help) and be enabled to appropriate its truths. (This will be discussed further in chapter 10.)

It is clear from these facts that illumination is more than some flash of mental insight or intuition. Espousing a low, faulty view of illumination, Randolph Miller writes, "The Holy Spirit provides the gift of *illumination.* This may be the inner light . . . the warmth of heart . . . the intuition granted to a scientist, the moment of truth which comes to all of us when we see clearly what the truth is for us. We ascribe this gift to the Holy Spirit because we can never predict the moment when the light will come down."[38]

How does illumination relate to the teaching work of the Spirit? Some think His teaching and His illumination are identical. Others prefer to think of teaching as broader, including both revelation and illumination. In a sense, illumination is revelation of a sort. But strictly speaking, biblical revelation is the communication of God's truth in written form, while illumination is the communication of the *meaning* of truth. However, the Spirit in illumination is not creating *new* truths. He has communicated the truth, once for all recorded infallibly in the Bible. Now, rather than giving new truths, He guides into truth already revealed. Of course, to the believer being illumined, the truths may be new, if he has never before known them. Only in this sense is illumination an aspect of revelation.

The Spirit's work of revelation (giving an objective body of truth, the Bible) was completed when the last words of the Bible were inspired. But He now works on the written Word, making it a part of believers' lives.

In teaching, the Holy Spirit operates on (or activates) both the written Word and students: one He animates and the other He illuminates. Teaching, then, is the broader term and includes the revealing and animating of the Word, along with the illuminating of the hearts and minds of believers.

From this study of the Holy Spirit as a Teacher, it is seen that *teaching is no minor phase of the Spirit's work.* As the Spirit of truth, He gives understanding, wisdom, counsel, and knowledge; He imparts and appropriates truth; He teaches and guides believers into all God's revelation; He reminds of Christ's teachings; He announces things to come; and He reveals God's truth to humankind. He convinces sinners of their guilt; He anoints or indwells believers so that they need not rely on inadequate sources for learning God's truth; and He illumines the minds and hearts of believers to enable them to welcome and apply God's Word.

WHAT DO YOU THINK?

1. Some religious groups claim today that God has revealed Himself to us in writings other than the sixty-six Bible books. Why is this notion wrong?
2. Are Christians "inspired" today in the same way the Bible's human authors were inspired? How do they differ?
3. What differences do you see between the Bible's revelation and its inspiration?
4. What differences do you see between the Holy Spirit's inspiration of the Bible and His teaching ministry?
5. What is the anointing of the Holy Spirit, and how does it relate to His teaching ministry?
6. What are some wrong ways people have interpreted 1 John 2:27a, "And you do not need anyone to teach you"? Why are these views inadequate? How would you defend the view that this statement means we should not follow the views of false teachers?
7. As you study the Word in your lesson preparation, do you pray that the Holy Spirit will illumine your heart, that is, enable you to perceive and receive the truth?

PART TWO
TEACHERS AND
THE TEACHER

Because the Holy Spirit is the Teacher of God's truth, what part do human teachers have in Christian teaching?

Does the teaching ministry of the Holy Spirit eliminate the need for human teachers? Does the work of teachers in Christian education imply that the Spirit alone is insufficient to teach truths and change lives?

Is Christian education merely a human process, leaving no room for the Holy Spirit? Are Christian teachers left to their own human resources? Is the Holy Spirit not in need of human teachers, since His work is divine?

If human teachers and the Spirit are to work together, what is the distinct functioning of each? What does God do in teaching that teachers cannot do? What are teachers expected to do, and for what does God hold them responsible? How can the divine and the human cooperate in their teaching responsibilities?

Whenever God has employed human instruments to accomplish His purposes, people have been puzzled to know, and have often misunderstood, how and why God works in such fashion. The human mind wonders, for instance, how God could have employed fallible human authors to compose an infallible book. The human mind has difficulty comprehending how God could have employed a fallible human being—a virgin—to give birth to an infallible person, the incarnate Christ. So it is in teaching. How does God employ human teachers in a divine process to change lives?

CHAPTER 5
FALSE VIEWS ON THE DIVINE
AND HUMAN TEACHERS

SOMEONE HAS HUMOROUSLY REMARKED that there are two kinds of people who should never say "Oops": dentists and magicians. If a dentist's drill slips, it could seriously injure the patient's mouth. And if a magician botches a trick, his career may be jeopardized.

Of greater consequence than these blunders, however, are errors in the spiritual realm. Yet in doctrinal matters many false ideas abound. And the doctrine of the Holy Spirit's teaching ministry is no exception. Wrong notions about the Spirit's teaching role can result in weakened ministries. So we need to be sure we are skirting these four erroneous concepts.

THE HOLY SPIRIT EXCLUDES HUMAN TEACHERS

"I don't need to attend a Bible class or read Bible study helps, because the Holy Spirit teaches me directly. Why should I rely on a human teacher when I have the divine Teacher?"

This view implies that God's teaching is hindered, not helped, by human instructors. Taken to its logical conclusion, this notion says Christians never need to study, go to school, or learn from someone else. Since the Holy Spirit teaches Christians directly, all education, some argue, is unnecessary.[1] In this view, methods of teaching, educational materials, and programs are considered efforts of the "flesh" and are fallible, "worldly," and deficient. Any effort of human beings to transmit God's living truth only contaminates and trespasses on the priority of the Holy Spirit.

Sometimes even Bible-believing Christians fall victim to this kind of false thinking, supposing that education is actually an enemy of spirituality.

Some people adhere to this concept to cover their own deficiencies in learning ability or in educational training. Others maintain such a view as an indirect means of calling attention to their own supposedly superior spiritual state, which, they say, enables learning to stem directly from the Spirit. Others maintain this view because of an overly cautious concern that Christianity be guarded against the extremes of intellectualism, dead orthodoxy, or liberal education.[2]

The following facts argue against this view:

First, even in biblical times, God used human teachers to impart His truth to others. Christ's Great Commission includes the command to teach (Matt. 28:19–20). The early church leaders were engaged in a ministry of teaching and preaching (Acts 5:42; 15:35; 18:11; 28:31). Apollos taught others the things of the Lord (18:25), and Timothy was commanded to entrust the Word to "reliable men" who could then "teach others" (2 Tim. 2:2).

Second, the fact that God has given some believers the gift of teaching and has given gifted leaders to the church is evidence that He uses human instruments to communicate His truth (Rom. 12:6–7; 1 Cor. 12:28; Eph. 4:11).

Third, the writer of the Book of Hebrews told his readers that they should be teaching others (Heb. 5:12).

Therefore it is wrong to suppose that the work of God's Spirit necessarily excludes His working through Christian teachers to lead others to the truth of God's Word. Though it is true that the Spirit can and often does teach believers directly, apart from human teachers, this possibility is not the point under discussion. The issue is not whether God *can* work alone but whether he *does*. God can work in sovereign grace independently of us, though He seldom chooses to do so.

THE HOLY SPIRIT SUBSTITUTES FOR HUMAN EFFORT

The erroneous concept that the Holy Spirit substitutes for human effort is somewhat similar to the previous false view. But whereas the former totally excludes the necessity of teachers, this view excludes only the need for preparation, study, or effort on the part of teachers. As Findley Edge explains, "There are those teachers who seem to feel that because they are teaching the Bible they do not have to know or follow proved educational principles. They do not want to be bothered with these 'new-fangled' ideas. Their attitude, simply stated, is 'I just teach the Bible and let the chips fall where they may.'"[3]

Those who have this attitude maintain that little or no training or preparation is needed, because, in the final analysis, the results in teaching come from the Holy Spirit.

This viewpoint is faulty for three reasons.

First, it is based on a wrong concept of teaching. In good teaching, the teacher is more than a "presenter" of truth; he is concerned about doing all he can to help develop lives, to lead students to Christlike living, all by means of the Holy Spirit. As Clarence Benson has suggested, "The *object* of our teaching is to make something happen in the life of the pupil."[4] The teacher who is well prepared is the most efficient and can at the same time rely on the Holy Spirit to work *through* him in his students. Benson also wrote, "We believe and insist upon Spirit-filled teachers, but can we hope that the Holy Spirit will honor unnecessary and unwarranted ignorance? As teachers, we are only instruments upon which the Holy Spirit must play, but surely it will make a difference whether the instrument is in tune or not.... If our teachers are to be tuned instruments for God's use, ought they not to be prepared? We want Spirit-filled teachers, but the Holy Spirit is not honored by our ignorance or by our indolence."[5]

Second, those who hold this view fail to see that teaching is a divine-human process in which the teacher and the Spirit are jointly involved. If a teacher is not adequately prepared, the teaching process becomes ineffective and learning is hampered. Though the Spirit may teach individuals in spite of the inadequacies of the teacher, more learning can take place when the teacher is prepared, and dependent on his Teammate, the Holy Spirit. "Surely the Lord can use to better advantage teachers who are thoroughly equipped for their work than those who are not."[6]

Third, this viewpoint, rather than magnifying the Bible and emphasizing the power of the Holy Spirit, borders on presuming on God "because it seeks to make God do what He is not supposed to do."[7]

The question may be asked, "Is it possible, then, for Christian teachers to depend too much on the Holy Spirit?" The answer is no, if teachers depend on the Spirit for spiritual enablement, for guidance as they prepare to teach, for illumination of their minds and hearts, for spiritual direction. The answer may be yes, if the teachers are supposedly depending on the Spirit to the exclusion of preparing their own hearts and minds for class sessions. So you should not ask or expect God to do what He expects *you* to do.

Paul's statement in 1 Corinthians 3:6 argues for the fact that human effort is *coupled with,* not *substituted by,* the divine working of God Himself: "I planted the seed, Apollos watered it, but God made it grow." Christian teachers are responsible to find God's ways of working and then work with Him. We should not try to exploit the Holy Spirit's ministry as an excuse for our weakness, laziness, or ignorance.

THE HOLY SPIRIT ADDS A
SPIRITUAL FOOTNOTE TO TEACHING

Another subtle, false idea about how the Holy Spirit teaches is that He adds a "footnote" or a blessing to whatever is taught. Some teachers seem to think Christian teaching is no different from secular teaching, except that they can ask God to bless their efforts. But this is not the way the Spirit operates in true Christian teaching. Teaching does not suddenly become Christian when a spiritual footnote is added to what the teacher imparts. Rather, biblical truth must be interwoven by the Spirit into the very fabric of teaching, if it is to be considered Christian education. As the Holy Spirit teaches, He does more than add a halo or appendix to what has been taught. His ministry is more than a mere taking over where we as teachers leave off.

To think of the teaching of the Spirit as an "annex" to our work is to overlook the fact that the Spirit teaches students before and during classroom situations, as well as afterward. Such thinking fails to see that the divine Teacher and human teachers are to work together as a team, simultaneously. When God is educating, the teacher and students are involved together in the teaching-learning process, and at the same time the Spirit is working *within* the teacher, *on* the Word of God, and *within* the learners.

THE HOLY SPIRIT IS TOTALLY UNNECESSARY

The view that the Holy Spirit is unnecessary is an extreme opposite of the first two views and is held by some who are involved in the task of religious teaching. Those who appreciate the importance of educational theory and practice, of methods and materials, of curriculum and equipment, sometimes tend to overlook the supernatural element so essential to dynamic Christian education.

They feel that if they are given the right set of methods, correct combination of learning situations, proper materials and environment, and ideal teaching-learning patterns, Christian learning and growth will naturally follow.

A neglect of the Spirit's ministry may also stem from the idea that such a consideration of the Holy Spirit is an attempt to understand the inscrutable workings of God. But, as LeBar explains, "Not that we should try to unscrew the inscrutable, but those things which God has revealed belong to us and to our children"[8] (Deut. 29:29). Others shy from viewing the Spirit of God as essential in Christian teaching because of an unwarranted fear that emotionalism may find its way into education. Pride in one's self-accomplishments in teaching may be still another reason why some disregard the necessity of the Spirit.

Three factors argue against such a view.

First, to think of the Spirit as unnecessary is to depend on the futile working of frail human efforts. If a person attempts to teach God's truths in his own power, he is wasting his time and energy in sterile unfruitfulness.

Second, this view tends to consider educational methods and procedures as ends in themselves. Methods are inherent in all that educators do, but it is wrong to be so taken up by the mechanics of Christian education that the essential dynamics of the workings of God's Spirit are overlooked. Some Christian teachers have faithfully followed sound educational principles and used excellent teaching techniques but have still been unsuccessful in teaching because they have not been guided and empowered by the Holy Spirit.

Third, this concept fails to consider the ultimate spiritual goals of Christian education. It overlooks the fact that God is the Teacher, and that pupils have needs that are far more than intellectual. Christian teaching seeks to do more than impart knowledge of truth to the head; it seeks to transform the life, by means of the Holy Spirit and the Word. Believers should desire the Word of God so that they "may grow," not merely know (1 Pet. 2:2). Hence the absolutely indispensable factor in Christian teaching is the inner working of God's Spirit in the lives of students, through His Holy Word.

TO THINK ABOUT

1. Why is it wrong to say, "Since the Holy Spirit is our divine Teacher, we don't need human teachers"?
2. If the Holy Spirit is our Teacher, why do we need to spend time studying and preparing our lessons?
3. What factors in Christian teaching make the role of the Holy Spirit essential?
4. As you prepare to teach, do you see yourself working as a partner in cooperation with the Holy Spirit? How can you cultivate that awareness to a greater degree?

CHAPTER 6
WHAT IS
THE GIFT OF TEACHING?

THE SUBJECT OF SPIRITUAL GIFTS is popular among many Christians. Yet many are confused. They wonder, "What are spiritual gifts? Why are spiritual gifts given? What is *my* spiritual gift? How do I discover my spiritual gift? When did I receive it? Do I have the gift of teaching?" Proper understanding of spiritual gifts, and particularly the spiritual gift of teaching, can enable us to perceive more accurately how the divine and human teachers should function together.

THE NATURE OF SPIRITUAL GIFTS

Before considering the specific gift of teaching, several general facts related to gifts may be considered.

First, the Scriptures make it clear that every believer has some gift. "To *each* one the manifestation of the Spirit is given for the common good" (1 Cor. 12:7, italics added here and in the following verses), and "All these are the work of one and the same Spirit, and He gives them to *each* one, just as He determines" (12:11). Gifts are given "as God has allotted to *each* a measure of faith" (Rom. 12:3, NASB). "*Each* one should use whatever gift he has received to serve others" (1 Pet. 4:10). "To *each* one of us grace has been given as Christ apportioned it" (Eph. 4:7).

In Scripture, spiritual gifts are often associated with the fact that believers are members of the body of Christ. Because each Christian is a member of Christ's body, he has been given a spiritual gift, however small or insignificant it may seem to be, to exercise in Christ's body. "In Christ we who are many form one body, and each member belongs to all the others" (Rom. 12:5). Christians "are the body of Christ, and each one . . . is a part of it" (1 Cor. 12:27), and Christ "gave gifts to men" (Eph. 4:8) "so that the body of Christ may be built up" (4:12).

Second, there is great diversity, and yet unity, among the gifts. "There are different kinds of gifts, but the same Spirit. There are different kinds of service, but the same Lord" (1 Cor. 12:4–5). The gifts differ according to the grace given to believers (Rom. 12:6). The lists of gifts (12:6–8; 1 Cor. 12:4–11, 28–30; Eph. 4:7–12) specify a great richness in the variety and diversity of gifts. Scholars differ on how many spiritual gifts are enumerated in the New Testament. Some say sixteen, others suggest nineteen, and others say twenty.[1]

Yet in this rich diversification there is uniformity and harmony, as indicated by the six occurrences of the word "same" in 1 Corinthians 12:4–6, 8–9, 11. "The one aim of these gifts is to minister to the unity of the body, for unity is wrought through diversity"[2] (Eph. 4:13, 16). Just as there are many parts to the physical body, so there are many members with varied gifts in the one body of Christ (1 Cor. 12:12, 14–20; Eph. 4:4).

Third, spiritual gifts are of divine origin, sovereignly bestowed by God. Each member is placed in the body of Christ with a particular gift or gifts, according to God's sovereign will. God "gives them to each one, just as *He* determines" (1 Cor. 12:11, italics added here and in the following verses), and "*God* has arranged the parts in the body . . . just as He wanted them to be" (12:18). These are "in accordance with the measure of faith *God* has given" (Rom. 12:3).

This fact should cause us not to covet spiritual gifts other believers possess. Instead, an attitude of humility should accompany the exercise of spiritual gifts, for they are all undeserved. Walvoord discusses the relationship of spiritual gifts to one's spirituality. "Because their bestowal is sovereign, it follows that it is not a question of spirituality. A Christian unyielded to the Lord may possess great spiritual value, while one yielded may have relatively minor spiritual abilities. It remains true, of course, that proper adjustment in the spiritual life of the believer is essential to proper exercise of his gifts, but spirituality does not bring spiritual gifts."[3]

God bestows gifts on believers because of His sovereign grace. It is interesting that the Greek word for "spiritual gifts" (charismata) is derived from the word for "grace" (charis).

Fourth, since every believer has a spiritual gift, one may conclude that the gifts are given at salvation. Nowhere did Paul or Peter infer that some believers receive a spiritual gift at salvation and that others are without such a gift and need to ask God for one.

But what about Paul's statement to Timothy that his gift was received "through the laying on of my [Paul's] hands" (2 Tim. 1:6)? And didn't Paul tell Timothy in 1 Timothy 4:14 that his gift was given "through a prophetic message when the body of elders laid their hands on" Timothy? As McRae suggests, Timothy's situation may have been a special case because Timothy was a delegate of an apostle, Paul.[4] Apparently God told Paul through direct revelation ("a prophetic message") that Timothy was to be given special apostolic authority. Therefore Paul (2 Tim. 1:6) and other elders (1 Tim. 4:14) laid their hands on Timothy, at which time he received a spiritual gift. The laying on of hands accompanied the reception of the gift; the hands were not the source of the gift. The gift came from God. (Laying hands on another person was an act symbolizing identification with the individual and the bestowal of authority on him; Num. 8:10; 27:18; Acts 6:6; 9:17; 13:3.) This, then, is a unique case not to be repeated today.

Fifth, some gifts are permanent, while others were temporary, having been exercised only in the apostolic age. The gifts possessed by some believers in the church today are teaching, evangelism, pastoring, exhorting, giving, showing mercy, helping, and faith. Among the temporary gifts are apostleship, prophecy, performing miracles, healing, tongues, and interpreting tongues. Walvoord cogently demonstrates the temporary nature of these latter gifts.[5] Also McRae, Gromacki, Dillow, and Lightner have helpful discussions on why some gifts were temporary.[6] The spectacular (sign) gifts authenticated the message of the apostles (2 Cor. 12:12; Heb. 2:3–4).

Sixth, spiritual gifts are given so that the body of Christ may be edified. Each gift is to be exercised for the profit and benefit of others. "Now to each one the manifestation of the Spirit is given for the common good" (1 Cor. 12:7). Gifts were given "to prepare God's people for works of service, so that the body of Christ may be built up" (Eph. 4:12).

Paul was anxious that spiritual gifts be used for *edification* (1 Cor. 14:4–5, 12, 26). Spiritual gifts are given not for the outward display of individual abilities but for the practical purpose of equipping the saints for ministering to the body of Christ. "Unity and utility define the aim of all the gifts and prescribe their legitimate exercise."[7]

THE NATURE OF THE GIFT OF TEACHING

The gift of teaching is one of the major gifts, for it is included in each of the three lists of gifts in the New Testament (Rom. 12:7–8; 1 Cor. 12:28; Eph. 4:11). Its importance is also highlighted by the fact that it is frequently mentioned along with the apostolic gift of prophecy (Acts 13:1; Rom. 12:6–7; 1 Cor. 12:28–29; Eph. 4:11). Since the temporary gifts of apostleship and prophecy were necessary only in the transitional phase of the apostolic age, the gift of teaching may be considered one of the first in the rank of permanent gifts for today (1 Cor. 12:28). (Not that some gifts are more essential than others [12:14–18], but some seem more prominent than others [14:2–4, 19].)

Teaching was also closely associated with preaching (Acts 5:42; 1 Tim. 2:7; 2 Tim. 1:11)[8] and is closely linked with the gift of pastoring. In Ephesians 4:11 the Greek words for "pastors" and "teachers" are closely linked. Also the word translated "some," occurring before the word "pastors," is omitted before the word "teachers." This implies that one cannot be a true pastor without also being a teacher. One way a pastor or shepherd cares for his flock is by teaching them. The pastor-teacher compares to the "teaching priest" of the Old Testament (2 Chron. 15:3).

Teaching is a vital part of the church because Christianity has a body of truth to transmit.

After three thousand people were saved on the Day of Pentecost, "they devoted themselves to the apostles' teaching" (Acts 2:42). Throughout the Book of Acts the apostles were engaged in teaching. After an angel released Peter and John from prison, "they entered the temple courts . . . and began to *teach* the people" (5:21, italics added in this and the following verses), and someone reported to the Sanhedrin that the men who had been put in jail were "*teaching* the people" (5:25). The apostles were then brought to the Sanhedrin and were released (5:27, 40). Then "day after day . . . they never stopped *teaching*" (5:42). "Barnabas and Saul . . . *taught* great numbers of people" in Antioch (11:26). In Corinth, "Paul stayed for a year and a half, *teaching* them the Word of God" (18:11). And in Ephesus, Paul "*taught* . . . publicly and from house to house" (20:20). In Jerusalem, the Jews charged that Paul was "the man who *teaches* all men everywhere" (21:28). Even when Paul was in Rome under house arrest, he "boldly . . . *taught* about the Lord Jesus Christ" (28:31).[9]

The teaching gift is primarily important in edifying the church, especially in the local church's Christian education ministry. Since gifts are given for ministering to the body of Christ, those who are most effective in this spiritual task of edification are those who possess and are cultivating the gift of teaching. Many seek to be teachers but achieve little spiritual success in their efforts because they do not have the teaching gift.

But what is the gift of teaching? Like other spiritual gifts, it is a supernatural ability. The gift of teaching is a supernatural, Spirit-endowed ability to expound (explain and apply) the truth of God. Teaching differs from exhortation in that the latter is the ability to persuade and encourage others to do God's will, whereas teaching is the gift of systematically instructing and applying the doctrines (or teachings) of God's truth.[10] Though all believers in fellowship with the Holy Spirit are taught by Him, not all believers have the ability to teach others effectively. A Christian teacher with the gift of teaching does not necessarily know the Bible better than others, but the gift does enable him to impart more effectively what he does know.

How does the spiritual gift of teaching relate to the natural ability for teaching? Spiritual gifts clearly pertain to the spiritual birth of a believer rather than to his natural birth. This is clear for several reasons: (1) The Scriptures never speak of non-Christians possessing spiritual gifts. (2) Spiritual gifts are more than manifestations of human ability because they are called "gifts." (3) They are given for edifying the body of Christ, and therefore are related to believers' new natures. (4) Spiritual gifts are called manifestations of the Spirit (1 Cor. 12:7).

Does this mean, then, that all spiritual gifts are of a vividly supernatural nature? Does an individual who before salvation had no ability or interest in, say, teaching suddenly at salvation possess the gift of teaching? Or is it possible that believers who are given the gift of teaching are often those who have had some natural teaching ability before they were saved? Though the Bible does not answer these questions explicitly, scriptural illustrations seem to shed some light on this problem.

Oholiab, for instance, was by natural ability "a craftsman and designer, and an embroiderer" (Exod. 38:23). But for working on the tabernacle, God "filled him [and Bezalel and other craftsmen] with the Spirit of God, with skill, ability, and knowledge in all kinds of crafts" (31:3; 35:31) for "constructing the sanctuary" (36:1).

Before Paul was saved, he had been trained in the schools of his day. His natural abilities, along with his training, made him a capable teacher, orator, leader, and administrator. Interestingly, after salvation his spiritual gifts were in line with these natural gifts (1 Tim. 2:7). Even today many people with evident talents in a certain sphere have been used of God mightily in that same sphere after salvation. For example, persons gifted in administration before salvation often find that they can best build up the church by exercising the spiritual gift of administering. Thus it is clear that at least some spiritual gifts have a basis in natural talent. But this in no way minimizes the element of sovereign bestowal. It is still a work of God to enable believers to use their natural abilities to the glory of God in a spiritual sphere.

Since spiritual gifts are sometimes (if not often) in accord with natural gifts, then what is the difference between a natural ability before salvation and the same ability after salvation? Many Bible commentators agree that the difference lies in a spiritual enhancing or strengthening of the natural ability. Lenski makes this comment: "Some of these gifts have a natural basis in natural talents and abilities. The Spirit sanctifies and augments these talents for His high and blessed purpose."[11] Dewar states that natural abilities are greatly enriched when they are consecrated, whereas other gifts "are clearly supernatural and in no way are they dependent upon natural talents."[12]

Those spiritual gifts, then, that are in accord with preconversion natural abilities, are an enhancing of those natural gifts, a channeling of those abilities into spiritual spheres of ministry, and involve a "special quickening to accomplish the task."[13] And all three factors are involved: an enhancing, a channeling, and a quickening. In keeping with this viewpoint there seems to be no apparent reason why certain characteristics common to both a natural and a spiritual ability may not be evident in an individual before salvation. The fact that spiritual gifts are bestowed at the time of salvation does not rule out the fact that God may be preparing a person before salvation along certain lines, in keeping with the spiritual gifts God plans for him to possess and exercise after salvation. This may often be true of the gift of teaching. Believers who possess the teaching gift may often be those whom God has been preparing, before their salvation, in areas related to a teaching ministry. But this is not *always* the case. "It may be frequently observed that individuals with little natural talent are often used mightily of God when those with great natural talent, though saved, are never similarly used."[14] McRae vividly illustrates this crucial point. "Do not confuse the natural talent with the spiritual gift. Happy is the case when they overlap in the same person, but we should never assume that one is qualified to teach Sunday School because she is a public school teacher. Without the gift she could communicate the factual content of the Sunday School lesson but there would be little or no spiritual growth and blessing."[15]

Regardless of what is said about this difficult problem of the relationship between spiritual gifts and natural abilities, there can be no question about the divine origin and providential appointment of spiritual gifts. Whether the spiritual gift of teaching is given in accord with the natural ability of teaching, this gift has its origin in God and consists of a supernatural divine enablement to expound and impart the Word of God to others.

Is the gift of teaching essential for teaching secular subjects, or is it needed only by those teaching the Bible? Can regenerate teachers successfully teach subjects such as biology, music, or mathematics, without the spiritual gift of teaching?

Offhand it would seem that this gift would be needed for teaching only biblical subjects. However, a closer consideration of the problem and the issues involved indicates otherwise. For one thing, Scripture does not warrant a sharp line of demarcation between "secular" truth and "spiritual" truth. As Frank Gaebelein has stated, "All truth is God's truth."[16]

Of course revealed truth as recorded in the Bible is of higher importance than "natural" truth. But the latter is within the framework of God's truth and needs to be taught as such. From this standpoint Christian teachers must be just as divinely enabled for teaching history or music as for teaching the Bible, provided they are interested in teaching these truths from a Christian frame of reference. In fact, the difficult task of integrating some so-called secular subjects into a Christian framework may demand even more divine ability than the task of expounding the Bible.

Spiritual gifts are given to persons, not to occasions. Believers who have received the spiritual gift of teaching are to exercise it, not merely on some teaching occasions but in teaching any truth. Christian teachers should use every teaching opportunity to orient students in their study of the "secular" to a Christian worldview. They should relate the principles of God's Word and Christianity to every subject they teach—and to do this, they must possess and exercise the spiritual gift of teaching. To teach biology from a Christian perspective is to teach, in a sense, spiritual (or God's) truth. Christian teachers must be divinely enabled by God's Spirit to expound to others God's truth—whether "secular" or spiritual. Gaebelein comments on this point:

> The call, then, is for a wholly Christian world view on the part of our education. We must recognize, for example, that we need teachers who see their subjects, whether scientific, historical, mathematical, literary, or artistic, as included within the pattern of God's truth. It is one thing to take for ourselves the premise that all truth is God's truth. It is another thing to build upon this premise an effective educational practice that shows the student the unity of truth and that brings alive in his heart and mind the grand concept of a Christ who "is the image of the invisible God," by whom "all things were created," who

"is before all things," and by whom "all things consist," or hold together.[17]

THE FUNCTION OF THE GIFT OF TEACHING

How is the gift of teaching discovered? How should it be developed and exercised? And what does all this imply?

It is one thing to be given a spiritual gift, but it is another thing to know what that gift is. All believers possess at least one spiritual gift, but many are unaware of what their gift or gifts may be. Spiritual gifts bestowed by God on believers are permanent possessions. These gifts do not come and go.[18] The exercise or use of the gifts may be intermittent, but the possession of them is permanent.

The duty of each believer, in reference to spiritual gifts, is to discover what his or her gift is and then to develop and exercise it to the glory of God.

In a sense *all* believers are teachers. Believers are exhorted to "teach and admonish one another" (Col. 3:16). Elders and others who are "the Lord's servants" must be "able to teach" (1 Tim. 3:2; 2 Tim. 2:24). Timothy was told by Paul to commit to faithful men the things he had heard from Paul, so they in turn "will also be qualified to teach others" (2:2). And older women are to teach younger women (Titus 2:3–4). On the other hand, the special gift of teaching is bestowed only on some believers.

It is the duty of every believer to discover his gift. It is one thing to have the gift of teaching, but it is another to know it. It is conceivable that some believers possess the gift of teaching but are unaware of the fact, having never exercised the gift. Either they have not been instructed about the matter of spiritual gifts, or they are out of fellowship with the Lord and are thus incapable of receiving and appropriating spiritual truth.

How, then, may one determine if he has the gift of teaching? Several guideposts may be mentioned. As noted before, sometimes this gift is given in accord with the natural ability of teaching. Therefore if a person had a natural talent as a teacher before he was saved, he should consider whether this may be his spiritual gift for edifying Christ's body. It may or may not be.

Another means of determining whether one has the gift of teaching is to minister in several capacities in a local church and elsewhere. If one possesses the gift of teaching, either he or others or both may discover his latent ability, as he ministers in a teaching capacity.

Another token by which this gift may be determined is the evident blessing of God on one's teaching, which may be sensed by the individual or by others. Often, spiritual results and blessings evidenced in one's ministry are a divine indication that the believer has struck on his prescribed ministry to the body of Christ. All this applies to lay persons as well as to Christians in so-called full-time teaching capacities. Obviously you can't accurately ascertain God's intentions for you in this direction unless you are in the center of God's will, "filled with the Spirit" (Eph. 5:18).

To discover a spiritual gift is only the first step toward its effective use. As a believer lives in God's will, he is then in the proper spiritual condition for developing his gift of teaching. The exhortation to develop and increase the effectiveness of a person's gift is stated at least three times in the Bible. Twice Paul addressed Timothy about his spiritual gift. (Whether Timothy had the gift of teaching is not fully clear in Scripture.) "Do not neglect your gift. . . . Be diligent in these matters" (1 Tim. 4:14–15). "I remind you to fan into flame the gift of God, which is in you" (2 Tim. 1:6). "Fan into flame" is a good translation of the word *anazōpyrein* (used only here in the New Testament), a word that is rendered "stir up" in the KJV and NKJV and "kindle afresh" in the NASB. Timothy was to exercise his gift in the sense of fanning it into a flame. He was to kindle or rouse to the utmost his latent gift. He was to exercise it, not neglect it by letting it lie unused.

Exercising spiritual gifts is an act of stewardship. "Each one should use whatever gift he has received to serve others, faithfully administering God's grace in its various forms" (1 Pet. 4:10). A spiritual gift is an entrustment, as well as an enablement and an endowment. If a Christian has the teaching gift, he is responsible to care for it as a steward would his master's household. "However rich the gifts which God has bestowed upon us, they do not grow of their own accord, but need to be cultivated by our own personal care."[19]

Various means by which you may develop your gift of teaching are observing others who have the gift, getting training and schooling in how to teach, and gaining teaching experience. As a good steward of what God has sovereignly bestowed, you should do all you can to improve and make the best use of your spiritual gift.

Nothing is basically wrong or unspiritual in getting training and schooling to improve the gift of teaching. Anything that can be done to improve the use of your gifts to the glory of Christ and the edification of the church should be undertaken and is in harmony with the exhortation in 1 Peter 4:10.

Suppose someone raises the objection, "How can a teacher improve what God has done or given? When God imparts the gift of teaching, it is imparted perfectly. At that moment a teacher is as good a teacher as he will ever be. To try to improve what God has done is to mix mundane and human efforts with a spiritual gift." This may be answered in three ways.

First, experience shows that this objection is without basis. Usually when a person begins to teach a Sunday-school class he does not necessarily do his best. As a result of time and concerted effort, he improves. Teacher-training programs for lay people in local churches also help teachers improve their efforts.

Second, educational technique is not necessarily incompatible with the ministry of the Holy Spirit. If anything, the two go together, because God's plan in teaching is to use Christians—capable Christians—as instruments of the Holy Spirit. If God calls a man to preach, that calling does not exclude the need to study the science and art of sermon preparation and delivery. Christian teachers should learn all they can about how to be more effective in their important task. This may include the study of teaching techniques, educational theory, student characteristics and development, the process of learning, lesson preparation and evaluation, the use of teaching aids, and so on. It may involve visiting others' classes, observing how others teach, reading about teaching, or attending teachers' meetings and Christian education seminars. It should include gaining new insights into the truths of God's Word, the way God has made people act and think, how God causes people to learn, and how to communicate the truth of God effectively. The Holy Spirit works best through teachers who know these factors in the teaching-learning process and who work in cooperation with God in the process.

Third, developing one's teaching gift can in no way improve the quality or essence of what God has given. Development is simply for the purpose of enlarging the effectiveness of the gift. It is not a matter of adding inherent quality to the gift but rather of expanding its usefulness. It is not a matter of adding good to what is bad or only partially good but rather of adding growth to what is implanted, development to what is undeveloped, fruition to what is latent. The parable of the talents in Matthew 25:14–30 illustrates the importance, in God's sight, of effectively using what He has entrusted, rather than letting it lie dormant and passive. The man who buried his single "talent" was not rewarded, whereas those with five or ten "talents" saw their investments multiply and were rewarded by their master. If a Christian teacher is not interested in developing his or her gift, he or she is not a good steward and the effectiveness of that ministry is endangered.

Another fact concerning exercising the teaching gift should be highlighted. The Bible does not suggest that there are different gifts for specific age-groups, such as the gift of working with children or the gift of youth work.[20] However, it may safely be stated that the teaching gift, in some or perhaps most cases, may best be exercised with a certain age-group, because of the teacher's background, interests, aptitudes, and personality. This is not a matter of differing gifts but of varying outlets for the one gift of teaching.[21]

Is the spiritual gift of teaching always necessary? Don't some inherently have a natural inclination or knack for teaching? Christians who apparently have this natural inclination for teaching either have the spiritual gift and may not realize it, or are exercising a spiritual gift in accord with a natural ability in teaching. Or this knack may be the result of exercising the gift over a period of time, so that the gift is now used with more ease and skill.

Several implications stem from these truths about the gift of teaching.

1. Not everyone can teach the Bible. Not all Christians in teaching positions necessarily possess the gift of teaching. Therefore church leaders should select their teachers with care.
2. Every Christian should do his or her utmost to determine his or her spiritual gift, and then seek to be in a place of service where that gift can be developed and exercised, whatever it may be (1 Tim. 4:14; 2 Tim. 1:6).
3. Effective Bible teaching (in local churches and Christian institutions) depends on teachers who have the spiritual gift of teaching. If the

Holy Spirit has not given the gift of teaching to the one who is teaching, he will never be a spiritually effective teacher.

4. Local churches should do all they possibly can to help believers determine and develop their spiritual gifts. This may mean counseling lay persons as well as using them in various capacities of Christian service.

5. Teacher training courses, in-service training, leadership training, and other training programs have definite, though indirect, biblical warrant.

6. In-service assistant teaching or substitute teaching can be a means of helping Christians determine if they have the spiritual teaching gift before they are given full positions of leadership responsibility.

7. If teachers are ineffective, they either do not have the teaching gift, are not developing it, or are not in fellowship with the Lord.

8. The twofold goal of all spiritual gifts should always be borne in mind: edifying the body of Christ (Eph. 4:12) and ascribing glory to the Lord (1 Pet. 4:11).

9. Teaching God's truth should always be done in the power of the Spirit and in an atmosphere and attitude of love (1 Cor. 13:1–7; Eph. 4:15–16).

10. Church leaders repeatedly need to emphasize in their teaching and preaching this important doctrine of spiritual gifts.

CHECK YOURSELF

1. What spiritual gift or gifts do you sense the Lord has given you?

2. If you believe you have the spiritual gift of teaching, what factors lead you to that conclusion?

3. If you are not sure you have the spiritual gift of teaching, what can you do now to see if you have that gift?

4. Assuming you have the gift of teaching, what steps could you take in the next six months to develop or improve your teaching effectiveness? For additional ideas, could you discuss this matter with your pastor or others?

CHAPTER 7
DISTINCTIVE MINISTRIES
OF THE DIVINE AND HUMAN TEACHERS

T HE FACT THAT God dispenses to some believers the gift of teaching shows that He has designed that human instruments impart His truth to others. But what is the distinctive function of human teachers in the educational process? What is the distinctive ministry of the Holy Spirit? In teaching, what does God's Spirit do that we cannot do? What part do we have in teaching for which God holds us responsible? Since learning and growing in the Christian life is a divine process in the spiritual lives of believers, what place do human teachers have? Conversely, since Christian teaching is an educational task involving teachers and learners, in what sense can Christian education be called a supernatural process?

It is incorrect to emphasize the supernatural element in Christian teaching to the exclusion of the place of human instruments. It is equally wrong to stress the importance of the place of teachers to the exclusion of the divine work of the Spirit. Yet the two must not be thought of as so blended that the place and function of each is blurred. In Christian education the divine and the human should function distinctively, yet cooperatively, in four areas. These four areas pertain to the gift of teaching, the principles of teaching, the channel in teaching, and the Word of God.

THE DIVINE AND THE HUMAN
WITH REGARD TO THE GIFT OF TEACHING

The Holy Spirit dispenses the gift of teaching to those whom He sovereignly chooses, whereas the responsibility of a human teacher is to discover that gift and then develop and exercise it to God's glory. The Spirit unfolds the gift; the human teacher should use it. The Spirit dispenses the gift; the human teacher should discover and develop is.

THE DIVINE AND THE HUMAN
WITH REGARD TO THE PRINCIPLES OF TEACHING

It is entirely erroneous to suppose that teachers devise the laws of pedagogy. God, not man, created the principles of teaching and learning. God made people learn according to certain patterns of development and in response to certain factors. When educators state these principles of learning and development, they are simply pointing out what they have discovered, not what they have created. Therefore every Christian teacher should determine to learn God's principles for teaching and learning. As he does, he is functioning in cooperation with the Holy Spirit.

THE DIVINE AND THE HUMAN
WITH REGARD TO THE CHANNEL IN TEACHING

The Holy Spirit seeks to teach through human channels or instruments. Human teachers should seek to be under the full control of the Spirit, as clean and capable instruments. Effective Christian teaching takes place to the extent that teachers allow the Spirit to speak through them and use them because "the Christian teacher in the local church is the mouthpiece of the Holy Spirit."[1]

Teachers are not free to teach what they please, because in the final sense, it is not they who teach, but the Holy Spirit. As instruments of the divine Teacher, they teach what the Spirit of God has revealed in His Word.

Also the Spirit seeks to supply guidance, power, illumination, and insight to teachers, who have the responsibility of using this enablement. We are not to be lifeless, passive automatons. Instead we are to be active, dynamic, vital channels, usable by the Spirit. "The Holy Spirit does not violate an individual's personality, but rather enables the believer to exercise his ministry in a spiritually effective manner."[2] Nor does this imply that lesson preparation by teachers is no longer necessary. If anything, it increases our need for preparation, so that we may be led by the Spirit to meet problems, questions, needs, and comments that arise in the classroom.

Paul said, "God . . . works in you to will and to act according to His good purpose" (Phil. 2:13). He also wrote, "I labor, struggling with all His energy, which so powerfully works in me" (Col. 1:29). "It is our talent that the Spirit uses, our insights, our enthusiasm, our hands—but it is His use of them that makes all the difference between wasted blight and jumbo harvest."[3] What a privilege to be instruments of and yet colaborers with God the Holy Spirit! Christian teachers ought to thrill at the thought of having such a vital part in God's work.

Such a privilege demands that Christian teachers be filled by the Spirit of God. This adds divine dynamic and spiritual power to the ministry of Christian teaching.

Without the spiritual impact of a yielded life, our efforts are relatively futile. With it, our efforts can become marvelously fruitful.

THE DIVINE AND THE HUMAN
WITH REGARD TO THE WORD OF GOD

The Holy Spirit transforms experience by the written Word,[4] whereas the task of human teachers is to *proclaim* to others the Word and to *portray* it in their own experiences. Only the Holy Spirit of God is capable of reaching and molding students' inner beings. Only He can take the Bible and make it operative in the hearts and souls of others. LeBar expresses this beautifully: "No other teacher can be both an outer and an inner factor. No other teacher can get inside the pupil to perform a personal, intimate operation in the depths of his being. As God's active agent or method, the Spirit does subjectively within the pupil all that Christ has done objectively without. Educational method is simply finding out how the Spirit works and working with Him rather than against Him, as we so often do even with the best of intentions. As the human teacher works with the divine Teacher, the scriptural record becomes more than letters and sounds and words; it becomes the living voice of God speaking to the heart."[5]

Only the Holy Spirit can do this. But the place of Christian teachers is by no means ruled out. It is every teacher's responsibility to work with the Spirit and thus be used by Him to effect inner changes. Both the teachers' lessons and living should be such that the Holy Spirit can use them to apply truth and stimulate spiritual growth.

This raises the question, "Who applies the truth to learners? Do teachers? Do learners? Does the Holy Spirit?" Actually it may be said that all three "apply" the truth, but each in a different sense. Teachers have the responsibility of pointing out or explaining truths to be applied, as well as areas in their learners' lives where truth should be applied. Learners, on the other hand, apply truth in the sense that they see the need for the truth to be related to their lives, yield to the work of the Spirit, and receive the Spirit's ministry. The Holy Spirit, however, is the only One who can apply truth in the sense of personalizing it to individuals, or making it a part of their experience. *Teachers present the Word, students receive and appropriate it, the Spirit relates it to students and transforms lives by it.*

This is not to say, however, that we need to be concerned only about declaring the truth, without any concern for heart-needs of students. Teaching includes both declaring truth and guiding learners. It is erroneous to suppose that all we need to do is unfold Scripture and let the Holy Spirit apply it where needed. There is a dangerous half-truth in such a statement. True, the Holy Spirit does apply the truth that has been taught. But He does so only with truth that has been carefully chosen with relation to life-needs and in cases where the heart soil has been prepared to receive the seed of God's Word. Scriptural truths scattered indiscriminately will inevitably fall on stony ground, thorny ground, or "by the wayside." Bible truths chosen and presented by teachers on the basis of life-needs and on prepared "soul soil" can be used to the fullest by the Spirit (Matt. 13:3–9, 18–23). Kaiser forcefully addresses preachers on this point: "Yes, even when we have faithfully discharged our full range of duties as exegetes and when we have also pressed on to apply that exegesis by principlizing the text paragraph by paragraph into timeless propositions which call for an immediate response from our listeners, we still need the Holy Spirit to carry that word home to the mind and hearts of our hearers if that word is ever going to change men's lives."[6]

The intricate interweaving of the human and divine elements is evident in 1 Corinthians 2:1–4:2. For instance, we should teach not with brilliance of speech or intellect (2:1, 4) but in the "demonstration of the Spirit's power" (2:4). The human part involves setting forth spiritual truths in words (2:6–7), but the Spirit unveils things never seen (2:9–10), shares the deepest truths of God (2:10–12), and gives insight into God's ways (2:15–16). We share the truth (plant and water it), but God gives the growth (3:6). A Christian teacher is a temple (3:16) and a steward (4:2), but the Spirit indwells the believer.

This teaching process, involving both the divine and the human, implies that Christian teachers should fulfill these six responsibilities:

- Learn how God works in teaching (know teaching principles) and then work with God.
- Depend on the Spirit to guide you and empower your teaching. Education should always occur in dependence on God.
- Use and develop your spiritual gifts.
- Be concerned for your students' growth and development.
- Motivate your students and help them learn.
- Live exemplary Christian lives and be usable by the Spirit in guiding your learners.

In this educational partnership, in which the human teacher and the Holy Spirit each have distinctive functions, it must be remembered that in the final analysis, God is the Teacher. As human teachers we are limited. We must recognize that the ultimate objectives of Christian education cannot be achieved in their own power. Christian teaching is a divine work in which the teacher and guide is God Himself. He supplies the truth. He aids teachers in teaching the truth, and learners in learning it. Thus "Christian education is more than a human enterprise."[7] Every Christian teacher must grant that it is ultimately "God who makes things grow" (1 Cor. 3:7). Teaching, like any aspect of Christian service, is "not by might, nor by power, but by My Spirit, says the Lord Almighty" (Zech. 4:6).

However, if the Holy Spirit is operative in Christian teaching, then why do teachers often fail to teach and students often fail to learn? The answer is that God has chosen to work through imperfect human instruments. Of the four basic factors in Christian teaching—the Holy Spirit, the Word of God, teachers, and students—the first two are perfect and infallible, and the other two are fallible and imperfect. The first two are invariable, and the other two variable. Therefore if learning does not occur, it is the fault of either the teacher or the student, or both—not the fault of God's Spirit or God's Word.

Human teachers are in a key position, capable of either facilitating or hindering learning. *What* and *how* we teach are vitally important. And our lives are important too—as important as the truths we teach orally. As Benson has reminded Christian leaders, "The example of a consistent Christian life counts more toward helping others reach a higher standard than any amount of instruction."[8]

And Cairns writes: "The example of a radiant, honest, scholarly personality must accompany this basic practical as well as theoretical intellectual theistic orientation. Students usually remember the teacher long after the data of the subject have been forgotten."[9]

This is not to belittle for a moment the absolute necessity of God's Word. Without it, Christian education is impossible. But it is to say that Bible truths should be taught and communicated through lives that exemplify the Word and exalt Christ.

Teachers whose lives are not yielded to the Holy Spirit and in whom there is unconfessed sin prevent the effective teaching ministry of the Spirit through them. Sin will hamper both the power of their influence *with* their students and the effectiveness of their presentation of truth *to* their students. Many teachers have admitted that at times their teaching has not been well received simply because of sin in their own lives. Even though all other factors in the teaching situation may be conducive to learning, sin in teachers' lives decreases the possibility of learning. Even when Christian teachers possess the gift of teaching, the extent of their effectiveness depends on their being controlled by the Holy Spirit. No doubt you too have sensed the difference in your teaching when you are filled with the Holy Spirit and when you are not.

Every teacher should so live and teach that he can testify as did the apostle Paul concerning his ministry among the Thessalonians: "Our gospel came to you not simply with words, but also with power, with the Holy Spirit, and with deep conviction. You know how we lived among you for your sake" (1 Thess. 1:5). This verse outlines the pattern every teacher should follow in his or her teaching ministry. The teacher's *content* ("our gospel," the Word), the teacher's *communication* ("with power," "with the Holy Spirit," "with deep conviction"), and the teacher's *conduct* ("how we lived among you")—all three are important. What you teach, how you teach, and how you live should harmonize to make your ministry scriptural and dynamic.

If you are teaching a scriptural portion, you should have experienced or should be experiencing this truth yourself. Or if you are teaching a so-called secular subject, you ought to have experienced or be experiencing the implications of the Christian viewpoint on that subject.

It is important that Bible truths be a part of teachers' lives so that they will know whereof they speak, will be concerned about the truth they are teaching, and will make an impact on those they teach. Lessons that make an impact on learners' lives are those that have first made an impact on the lives of teachers. If teachers delve into truth without relating it to their own spiritual experience, their students may see little need for living the truth. Many teachers in this way limit the Spirit's working through them.

Christian teachers must be in vital union with Christ. Their personal acquaintance with and deep love for Christ and His Word are essential. This must be ranked above their knowledge of things, books, or people.

These words addressed by Paul to Timothy should be pondered by every Christian teacher: "Watch your life and doctrine closely" (1 Tim. 4:16). It is not enough for teachers to be concerned only with their lives or only with the doctrine they teach. They must be concerned with both. This responsibility is basic to harmonious cooperation between the human and the divine in the glorious ministry of Christian teaching.

ASK YOURSELF

1. After reading this chapter, can you recall the distinctive roles of the Holy Spirit and yourself as teachers?
2. How would you express the separate roles of the Holy Spirit, yourself, and your students in relation to applying the Word?
3. If a student is not learning and applying God's Word, whose fault is that?
4. What reasons can you give for living out God's truth in your life? What might result from failing to do so?
5. How would you evaluate the statement, "Christian education is more than a human enterprise"?

PART THREE
THE HOLY SPIRIT AND
THE BIBLE

What place should the Bible have in Christian education? What should be the final authority in Christian teaching? What should be the center of the curriculum? Should evangelical teaching be transmissive or progressive? If teachers are teaching in cooperation with the Spirit, does this mean that their interpretations of the Bible are accurate?

CHAPTER 8
THE BIBLE AS THE AUTHORITY
FOR CHRISTIAN EDUCATION

I ENJOY READING murder mysteries, both fictional and real. It's fascinating to try to determine who committed the murder, especially when several people could seemingly be guilty. Sometimes some unusual legal circumstance arises, which calls for the attorneys to consult their law books for an authoritative answer to their dilemma. A court case may even be delayed for a few hours or days to give attorneys time for additional research in their legal libraries. These written sources stand as authoritative guides on how they should proceed.

Teachers too need an authoritative voice, a final source of authority that tells, in essence, what they should teach and what their students should believe and how they should live. What criterion or standard should teachers follow in determining the material to teach and the activities in which to engage their students? What authoritative guide should learners accept in testing the conflicting voices that seek to tell them what to believe and do? What should be the final voice of authority in Christian education? Should it be the church? Teachers? Students' experiences? The Holy Spirit? The Bible?

Because "the problem of authority is the most fundamental problem that the Christian church ever faces,"[1] Christian teachers need to consider this problem carefully. There are currently several views about authority in evangelical teaching.

THE CHURCH AS AUTHORITY

Some people claim that the final authority for faith and life is the official teaching of the institutional church. This view is held by Roman Catholics and a few Protestant groups.

The Roman Catholic Church accepts the Bible as authoritative but insists that it alone is not a safe guide. Oral tradition supplies what is lacking in written tradition, the Scriptures, and thus is an authority alongside the Bible. Church tradition is authoritative because it testifies to the inspiration and preservation of Scripture, and because it was appealed to by church fathers to refute heresies and settle controversies.[2] To Roman Catholics, the church is the final authority because it is the custodian, guardian, teacher, and interpreter of the Bible, and the custodian and preserver of oral tradition. The church is the interpretive authority in all matters of faith and morals, and its pronouncements must be accepted without question.

The following arguments speak against the doctrine that church tradition, whether written or oral, has final authority:

First, ecclesiastical tradition often contradicts itself, thus destroying its claimed authority.

Second, church tradition often contradicts Scripture. This then necessitates a choice of one or the other as final and authoritative. Since church tradition is often self-contradictory, it is obvious that Scripture stands as sole authority over tradition.

Third, tradition places the church above the Bible. But the church as a corporate body or council did not give the Bible to the world. God gave the Bible, but He used individuals, not a hierarchy or an institution, to pen His inspired Word. "Calvin insisted that the church is governed by the Word and the Spirit, and therefore must be in subjection to the Scriptures. All traditions and the entire ecclesiastical hierarchy must submit to this lordship."[3]

Fourth, church tradition cannot be the final authority for Christian education because it is based on human opinions, not divine revelation. Calvin highlighted this fact by saying that "our faith would have too weak a foundation if we had only the authority of men."[4] He opposed ecclesiastical authority because it makes the truth of God dependent on "the arbitrary will of men."[5] The voice of the church concerning Scripture, no matter how dogmatic it may claim to be, is still the voice of humans, not God.

TEACHERS AS AUTHORITY

Another approach to the problem of authority is the view that teachers and scholars are the voice of final authority in matters pertaining to Christian living and Christian education. They are the final determinants and guides in structuring an educational curriculum. J. I. Packer describes this position. "Just as the medievals tended to equate church tradition with the Word of God, so modern Protestants tend to equate the words of scholars with the Word of God. We have fallen into the habit of accepting their pronouncements at second hand without invoking the Spirit's help to search Scripture."[6]

Teachers of this kind tend to suppress student expression. This was one of the chief complaints John Dewey (1859–1952) voiced against traditional secular education. This complaint applied equally well to Christian education. According to Dewey, "The traditional scheme is, in essence, one of imposition from above and from outside. It imposes adult standards, subject matter, and methods upon those who are growing . . . toward maturity. . . . The very situation forbids much active participation by pupils in the development of what is taught. Learning here means acquisition of what already is incorporated in books and in the heads of the elders. Moreover, that which is taught is thought of as essentially static."[7]

Though Christian educators do not accept many of Dewey's concepts, they do recognize that his complaint merits some thoughtful consideration.

For teachers to prescribe what pupils shall uncritically accept is to border on authoritarianism. Christians do have an *authoritative* message, but that should never be confused with an *authoritarian* method. LeBar clarifies this distinction:

> The major problem in relation to authoritative revelation is to get it accepted by each new generation. This acceptance cannot be forced, it must not be superficial. *Authoritarian* method is often associated with our *authoritative* message. If the Bible is taught in the

spirit of "Here it is; you take it because I say so"; if it is taught by stereotyped, rote-memory methods, what happens? Instead of accepting it as their own conviction, young people rebel against this affront to their free will. Likewise we fail if we try to transmit Scripture by transmissive methods, if we only ask young people to parrot it back to us in the form in which we gave it.[8]

The idea that teachers or scholars are the authority in education borders on authoritarianism, tends to stifle creativity and learning, and makes the acceptance of truth superficial.

EDUCATIONAL EXPERIENCE AS AUTHORITY (PROGRESSIVE EDUCATION)

According to John Dewey, the authoritative norm in education is the learners' experience. He did not discard authority altogether; he simply shifted the source of authority from the teacher to the learners. Dewey advocated learning through experience rather than from textbooks and teachers. He stressed that the aim of education is the continuous "reconstruction" of experience; students' experiences are to build on previous experiences and are to shape their experiences that follow. Since experience is worth far more than theoretical knowledge,[9] the center of the curriculum should be the student's own social activities.[10] (He stressed relevance, problem-solving, participation, and creativity in the learning process—valid points [see chapter 11], but all based on faulty philosophical premises.)[11] Of course experience *is* a part of the educative curriculum, but it is erroneous from the evangelical viewpoint to hold that "education is a development within, by, and for experience"[12] and nothing more.

This view of experience in education stems from Dewey's underlying naturalism, in which he repudiated the belief in authoritative moral or spiritual truth.[13]

Dewey's emphasis on experience, along with later developments in the field of psychology, influenced religious educators to see the importance of understanding the response of the people being taught as well as the subject matter they were seeking to teach. In many circles this resulted in a shift of authority from subject matter to student experiences. "So religious education began to turn to curricula designed with the needs and abilities and experiences of its pupils as a guiding principle."[14] Thus some religious educators even went so far as to say that "the source of authority is in the educational process itself."[15]

To accept the experience of learners as the core of authority in education is to accept a subjective and therefore unreliable norm. It places education in the quagmire of experimentalism and leaves students without any infallible source of truth.

Christian education involves far more than experience; it begins with the supernatural message of God's truths, His infallible written revelation, the Bible. The Bible is God's objective revelation of Himself and His purposes to humankind. It is His communication by which He seeks to transform us into Christlikeness, on the basis of salvation through faith in Christ. The Bible is the judge of educational experience, not vice versa. Therefore in Christian education, experience alone cannot be the final court of appeal.

RELIGIOUS EXPERIENCE AS AUTHORITY (LIBERALISM AND NEOLIBERALISM)

According to liberalism, God contacts man through religious experience. In his subjective religious faculties, a person knows God and thus his final authority is within his own soul.

The specific essence of religious experience may be feeling (Friedrich Schleiermacher), valuation (Albrecht Ritschl), filial piety or prayer (Auguste Sabatier), or ecstasy (mysticism), but in and through this subjective experience God gives Himself.[16]

Sabatier expresses the sentiments of religious liberals regarding the authoritative nature of religious experience and reason: "Moses, Isaiah, Paul, John, Peter, are to me and will continue to be, in the religious order, men of God clothed with a very great moral authority; I put myself to school with them, I profit by their lessons, they are incomparable models and previous teachers; but, after all, I am still free to choose between their ideas, to criticize their reasonings, to reject such of their teachings as are to me unassimilable."[17]

Millar Burrows accepts the principle that "what is ultimately authoritative for us is that which commands the assent of our own best judgment, accepted as the witness of the Spirit within us."[18] This view leaves us without any evaluative norm of judgment, without any intelligent basis for faith, without any final, objective authority. Each person accepts as authority what is right in his own eyes.

EXISTENTIAL ENCOUNTER AS AUTHORITY (NEOORTHODOXY)

Neoorthodoxy implies that a person's subjective response to God's revelation is the ultimate determinant of spiritual truth. Neoorthodoxy maintains that authority is not in the Bible and that the Bible is not the Word of God unless it is met by the existential response of individuals in a divine-human encounter. The Bible is simply a record of revelation and becomes the Word of God only when it speaks to the human soul. God does not give propositions of truth about Himself; He reveals Himself. The Bible is not revelation; it becomes revelation only when a person responds to God's encounter in which He, not information about Himself, is revealed.

Because one's response to the record of revelation supposedly guarantees the Bible's validity, that person becomes his own standard for determining what in the Bible is the Word of God. He stands in judgment on the Bible; and therefore his experience, not the Bible, is his authority or guiding principle.

According to neoorthodoxy the Bible is both "witness" and "instrument." As witness it is the record of God's past revelatory events, and as instrument it is the revelatory means whereby God today speaks His Word.[19] Karl Barth says the Holy Spirit prepares people to receive revelation as God's Word. As the "finger of God," the Holy Spirit is "the subjective aspect in the conception of revelation"[20] by which His Word becomes truth to man. George Schreyer explains that "the Bible is *a record* of experiences of the early Hebrews and Christians in *their* response to God and God's disclosure to them."[21] Also the Bible is "an instrument of God."[22] Rachel Henderlite speaks of the Bible as both a record of and witness to revelation.[23] She adds that at the same time the Bible is revelation; nevertheless in true neoorthodox fashion she thinks of revelation as events, not propositions.[24] The Bible is not inerrant, she argues,[25] and it is not to be thought of as a "repository of utterances of the Holy Spirit."[26] Somewhat unusual is her view that authority lies not in Scripture nor in the church but in the Holy Spirit.[27] Her discussion of this view seems to suggest that teachers taught by the Holy Spirit are the authority.[28] As interpreter of the Scripture, the church becomes the authority.

The neoorthodox position of revelation and authority is unacceptable by evangelicals for the following reasons:

First, neoorthodoxy leaves us without a normative criterion of truth, setting us adrift on the sea of speculations and doubts. We are asked to accept the trustworthiness of a spiritual experience, based on an untrustworthy Bible record. As R. A. Finlayson argues, "We are left in the impossible position of having to accept as true as a matter of religious experience what we must reject as false as a matter of objective reality. In no other department of human thought or research is truth based on subjective experience that lacks objective reality, yet this is what is offered us as the basis of religion."[29]

Second, the idea of revelation as encounter borders on mysticism. The Bible serves only as the frame within which the Spirit existentially encounters people.

Third, divine authority cannot reside in a human, fallible Bible. If the Bible is a human, errant document, it cannot serve, with any degree of reliability, as a witness or instrument to point people to a personal knowledge of God.[30] At best all neoorthodox Christian educators can do is seek to encourage their students to respond to God's encounter.[31]

Fourth, neoorthodoxy has no way of guaranteeing that a person has actually received revelation from God.

THE BIBLE AS AUTHORITY (EVANGELICALISM)

Evangelicals have consistently maintained that authority ultimately rests with God. As Creator and Sustainer of the universe, He has the absolute right over all created beings and all-embracing authority in heaven and on earth. As the second person of the Trinity, Jesus Christ possesses divine authority. "All authority in heaven and on earth has been given to

Me" (Matt. 28:18). "He taught them as One who had authority" (Mark 1:22). This authority of God is expressed to individuals not through the church, nor religious experiences, but through divine self-revelation. Because God has revealed Himself through the Scriptures, the Bible is divinely authoritative, possessing divinely *delegated* authority. This is cause and effect: *The Bible is God's revelation to mankind, and therefore it has divine authority.*

The Bible is the special revelation of God in written, "God-breathed" form (2 Tim. 3:16). Both the Old and New Testaments are the written revelation of God. The Word of God and Scripture are identified as one (John 10:35). Revelation is identified with "the Scriptures of the prophets" (Rom. 16:25–26, NASB). Paul's epistles were recognized by Peter as coauthoritative with "the other Scriptures" (2 Pet. 3:15–16). In one verse Paul quoted from both the Old Testament (Deut. 25:4) and the New Testament (Luke 10:7) and referred to both passages as "Scripture" (1 Tim. 5:18).

Christ recognized the authority of the Old Testament as God's written revelation. "Until heaven and earth disappear, not the smallest letter, not the least stroke of a pen, will by any means disappear from the Law" (Matt. 5:18). "Do not think that I have come to abolish the Law or the Prophets" (5:17). "The Scripture cannot be broken" (John 10:35). Jesus' ministry, crucifixion, and resurrection were in fulfillment of the authoritative Old Testament.

The apostles also recognized the authority of scriptural revelation. "For everything that was written in the past was written to teach us" (Rom. 15:4). "These things happened to them as examples and were written down as warnings for us" (1 Cor. 10:11). The apostles quoted the Old Testament as the Word of God (Acts 4:25; Rom. 9:17); they recognized the authority of Christ's teachings (Acts 20:35; 1 Cor. 7:10); they claimed an authoritative commission from Christ (Gal. 1:1); they were joined in rank with the Old Testament prophets (2 Peter 3:2); and their God-inspired writings came from the authoritative voice of God (1 Cor. 14:37; Gal. 1:8; 1 Thess. 2:13; 2 Thess. 2:15; 3:14; 1 John 1:1–5).

Evangelicals accept the Bible as their authoritative guide and rule for faith and conduct because it is an objective revelation, an infallible norm, and the truth of God (John 17:17; 1 Thess. 2:13). The Bible gives us an absolute standard and test of truth. As such, it contains propositions of truth about God, and through the Holy Spirit it brings people into loving relationship with God. Whether someone receives the Bible as his or her authority does not affect the authoritative quality of the Bible. It stands as the infallible authority of truth, regardless of one's attitude toward it.

Archbishop William Temple rejects the concept of propositional revelation on several counts, one of which is that if Christians are to regard the Bible as a body of infallible doctrines, they need an infallible human interpreter to tell them what it means.[32] However, why should the Bible need an infallible interpreter when it is already infallible? Furthermore believers do have, in a sense, an infallible interpreter—the Holy Spirit. As the true church's infallible Teacher, the Holy Spirit guides believers into the meaning of Scripture and aids them in determining laws for interpreting it. Packer adds, "We measure all human pronouncements on Scripture by Scripture's own statements."[33] (For more on the Holy Spirit and interpretation, see chapter 10.)

Some teach that the Christian's authority is not Scripture, but Christ, who is above it as its judge. They say that Christians must judge Scripture by Him and accept only what is in harmony with His life and teachings. Herbert Framer calls "the living Christ speaking through the Holy Spirit"[34] the final and absolute authority for the faith and life of the church. And Lewis Grimes states that "the pivot of authority is the event of Jesus Christ— God entering into and acting through history to speak a living word to man's questions and needs."[35] This view is unsatisfactory for the following reasons:

First, it leaves us without an objective means of ascertaining Christ's voice of authority. The Bible is the only adequate source by which we may gain an understanding of God. As George Fisher observes, "If it be alleged that Christ is the one Authority, yet it is through a critical study of the Scriptures, apart from subjective prejudice, that the knowledge of Christ is to be obtained."[36]

Second, Christ used His personal authority to confirm the authority of the Old Testament. Christ is the ultimate Authority, but it is through the Bible that He now exercises His divine authority, imparting authoritative truth. The Bible is clothed with His authority. Therefore in a sense both

Christ and the Bible are our authority. Packer cogently argues this point. "Certainly, He is the final authority for Christians: that is precisely why Christians are bound to acknowledge the authority of Scripture. Christ teaches them to do so. A Christ who permits His followers to set Him up as the judge of Scripture, One by whom its authority must be confirmed before it becomes binding and by whose adverse sentence it is in places annulled, is a Christ of human imagination, made in the theologian's own image, one whose attitude to Scripture is the opposite to that of the Christ of history."[37]

Another question is sometimes raised in reference to the Bible's authority: "Don't the Holy Spirit and the Bible together comprise a dual authority?" Ramm's answer is in the affirmative: "The Holy Spirit speaking in the Scripture . . . is the principle of authority for the Christian church."[38] But this view leads to the idea that if the Holy Spirit does not speak in the Bible, the Bible is not authoritative. As previously noted, the Bible *alone* is fully authoritative, because it is God's inspired revelation. This was the Reformers' position on *sola scriptura*.

With Ramm it is agreed that the *pattern of authority* consists of Christ, the Word, and the Holy Spirit,[39] but this must not convey the notion that the Word does not bear authority apart from the Holy Spirit. When the Spirit is joined with the Word, He does not *give* it authority; He appropriates the truth to us, and thus makes the Word of God effective in our hearts. The authority of the Word is then recognized by the believer. The Spirit witnesses to this authority, but He does not give authority to the Bible. As J. N. Thomas explains, "The Spirit does not *constitute* the authority but rather *testifies* to its authority."[40]

The divine authority of the written Word is the "distinctive mark of true Christianity"[41] and the only basis for an adequate curriculum in true Christian education. Education that bypasses the final authority of God's Word is not evangelical Christian education. Otherwise each student is left to carve his own path through the labyrinth of ideas in the search for truth.

The Bible is more than a resource among resources "to be used in validating and evaluating the sources of encounter with God."[42] Instead, it is the only authoritative norm in Christian education and the foundation and basis of all Christian teaching.

Because we accept God's scriptural revelation as our ultimate authority, it follows that it is the primary source of the guiding principles for Christian education.

We are amiss if we borrow principles of education from sources such as reason, experience, or humanly devised educational systems. God's distinctive revelation—the Bible—is the ultimate source from which educational principles should be drawn. LeBar laments that failure to do this has resulted in lack of spiritual reality in Christian teaching: "A chief reason for the lack of life and power and reality in our evangelical teaching is that we have been content to borrow man-made systems of education instead of discovering God's system. Secular educators do not give central place to the unique revelation of God's Word that is communicated by God's Spirit. Our distinctive content calls for distinctive treatment."[43]

Evangelical educators cannot accept secular education as its source of principles because it is often at variance with Scripture. Secular educational principles are often built on unscriptural philosophical bases such as pragmatism (truth is determined by what "works"), empiricism (truth is determined by our experience), and naturalism (truth is determined by science and nature). When there is conflict or variance in principles, Christian educators need to go back to their divine source to be sure the principles they have formulated are drawn from or are consistent with Scripture.

The Bible is not a textbook on education, but it does include insights into educational philosophy and method. Because God made the learner, his teacher, his content, and his environment, Christians look to God and His Word for valid educational concepts.

THINK IT THROUGH

1. What is wrong with saying church traditions are as authoritative as the Bible?

2. How do you evaluate John Dewey's emphasis on pupil experience?

3. How do you evaluate the teaching of neoorthodoxy that the Bible is not a revelation of God in itself but becomes revelation only when it subjectively encounters the human soul?

4. Why do evangelicals emphasize the authority of the Bible? How does its authority relate to its infallibility? What difference should the Bible's authority and inerrancy make in our teaching?

CHAPTER 9
THE BIBLE AS THE BASIC CONTENT
OF CHRISTIAN EDUCATION

B ECAUSE THE BIBLE is the authority for Christian education, it should be our ultimate source of educational principles. But it is also the essential content of Christian education. Too often, religious education has greatly neglected the place of content, as William Bower admits.[1] The content of the written Word of God is important because it makes plain God's will for humankind. Christian education concerns itself with Bible content because through it individuals can be brought into direct, personal contact with the living God.

For this reason, Christian education is transmissive, that is, it has truth to transmit or convey. *We have a Book to teach, God's divine Word to communicate, a written revelation to make known.* God's truths are not hidden in the inner recesses of human nature, to be drawn out by teachers. Nor are they there in seed form, merely waiting to be developed. God's truth is to be shared by teachers, as indicated in verses such as Exodus 10:2; Deuteronomy 6:6–9, 20; 31:11–13; Psalm 78:2–7; Luke 24:27, 32; Acts 8:4; 28:31; and 2 Timothy 2:2; 3:15.

The unregenerate are ignorant of God's truths. Their religious concepts are garbled by sin, and they are blind to the truth of God (Rom. 1:19–32; 1 Cor. 2:6–14; 2 Cor. 4:4; Eph. 4:18). Therefore this truth must be transmitted to them if they are to know Christ, who is the way, the truth, and the life (John 14:6).

The Bible is "propositional," containing statements or propositions of truth about God and His dealings with man. Those propositions are not written systematically in textbook form but are related to experiences recorded in the Bible. It is impossible for God to reveal Himself without revealing something of His character, attributes, or purposes. Biblical revelation is both propositional and personal, rather than simply one or the other. Propositional truths about God are revealed in the Bible, as indicated in 2 Samuel 7:27, where David prayed, "O LORD Almighty, God of Israel, you have revealed this to your servant, saying, 'I will build a house for you.' So your servant has found courage to offer you this prayer" (see also Isa. 22:14; Amos 3:7; Matt. 11:25; 16:17). Personal knowledge of God is stressed in Philippians 3:10, where the apostle Paul proclaimed, "I want to know Christ and the power of his resurrection and the fellowship of sharing in his sufferings, becoming like him in his death." But both truth about God and God Himself as a person are revealed in 1 Samuel 3:21: "The Lord continued to appear at Shiloh, and there he revealed himself to Samuel through his word."

Transmissive Bible teaching is decried by many schools of thought as unsound and unrealistic. It is claimed that transmitting Bible truth makes teaching noncreative, limits the content to a prescribed "given" body of content, and is irrelevant to learners' experiences. But divine authority demands human creativity. There is no reason why Bible teaching cannot be an exciting creative venture. The "given" truth in Christian education liberates persons into true Christian freedom (John 8:32). Furthermore, Christian truth is life-transforming. And it is "useful for teaching, rebuking, correcting and training in righteousness, so that the man of God may be thoroughly equipped for every good work" (2 Tim. 3:16–17).

The problem is that Christian teachers have not always indicated the Bible's relevance to life-needs and situations. Religious educators have spoken against transmissivism because to them it appears, as it did to George Coe,[2] to lead to or be identical with dead orthodoxy.

Many Christian educators must plead guilty to this charge. Transmissivism often does lead to dead orthodoxy simply because the teaching of God's truths has been attempted apart from the power of the Holy Spirit. The mere intellectual mastery of Bible truths does not guarantee spiritual living. The truth must become a part of the students' lives.

But this can take place only by means of the inner working of the Holy Spirit. Ludwig Haetzer, a sixteenth-century Anabaptist, stressed the need for the Holy Spirit's work in this way: "He who goes only by the Scriptures receives knowledge, but a useless knowledge, which does not reform. No man, no matter how learned he may be, can understand the Scriptures unless he [has] experienced and learned them in the depth of his soul. Otherwise men speak of the matter like a blind man [speaking] of color."[3]

Transmissive teaching has built-in power only because of the presence and work of the Holy Spirit. Ineffective transmissive teaching does not imply that teachers should discard Bible content. Instead, it means they should seek to teach Bible content in the power and dynamic of God's Spirit.

This brings to light two extreme positions of thought regarding authoritative content and personal experience. Some educators emphasize mastery of subject matter, whereas others stress the development of students. The former is generally referred to as traditional transmissivism and the latter as progressivism. In the former, content is vital, and students have presumably learned when subject matter is memorized, understood mentally, and can be reproduced in written form for the teacher. The goal of Christian education, according to this view, is familiarity with Bible facts.

Other teachers believe the curriculum should center exclusively on the students' experiences. With an eye to student needs, these educators tend to exclude any fixed content from the curriculum.

Neither of these extreme positions gives proper place to the Holy Spirit. An overconfidence in the ability of transmitted subject matter to bring about learning tends to neglect the work of the Spirit in the teaching process. Progressivism, on the other hand, magnifies the place of student experience to the extent that the Spirit of God in the educative process is deemed unnecessary or is overlooked.

Neither view is accurate. Neither content nor experience can be omitted or minimized with impunity. In evangelical Christian education both content and experience are necessary—with Bible content as the basis of the curriculum.

Experience is the avenue of interaction in the learning process, which is guided by the Holy Spirit. In Christian education, experience, when it involves the interaction of learners with the written Word and Christ, the living Word, takes on a supernatural nature.

But experience in education must have the right foundation. Experience not adequately based on the authoritative foundation of Scripture is empty mockery. With a wrong foundation, the possibility for right experience is canceled. This is one of the inadequacies of neoorthodoxy. Neoorthodox theologians are interested in personal experience with God rather than simply a knowledge of facts about God. This is fine. But they seek to gain this experience by means of existential encounter, apart from doctrinal truth. Thus they have no ground of objectivity and no assurance that their experience is valid.

According to the biblical view, a person comes to know God in experience as he or she knows truths about Him. *Experiencing God personally is possible only by first grasping facts about Him* (though the latter does not always guarantee the former). Our concepts about God lead us to knowing Him personally only as we are receptive to the ministry of the Spirit. For example, the more you understand that God is faithful and loving, the better you can trust Him with your future. Valid Christian experience (whether it pertains to spiritual birth into the Christian life or to growth within the Christian life) cannot be obtained or maintained apart from valid Christian truth.

In evangelical Christian education the curriculum is to be Christ-centered, Bible-based, and life-related.

The curriculum is to be Christ-centered in these senses:

First, Christ, the living Word (John 1:1), is central in the Bible, the written Word. He is the Savior, Lord, Friend, Advocate, and coming King on whom all Scripture focuses. Because Christianity is Christ, all Christian education should be centered and focused on Him.

Second, Christ is the goal of Christian living. Believers are "in all things to grow up into Him" (Eph. 4:15), to know Him (Phil. 3:10), to be conformed to His image (Rom. 8:29), to be mature in Him (Col. 1:28). Christlikeness is the goal toward which evangelical educators seek to lead their learners.

Third, Christ is the source of strength for Christian teachers. We must look to Him for spiritual sustenance, gracious enablement, divine power. Only in Christ can we know "His incomparably great power" (Eph. 1:19).

The curriculum is to be *Bible-based* in the sense that the Scriptures constitute the basic content for Christian education. All curricular materials and activities are to be faithful to and based squarely on the foundation of biblical truth. The Bible is the "given," the body of content to be transmitted. It is the "basis" of all evangelical Christian education. Edward Hayes stresses that the Bible is to be given a prominent place in the curriculum. "For if the Scriptures in original form are the only infallible record of Jesus Christ and if the Scriptures are the primary sources and only inerrant criterion of truth, then our commitment to educating men and women in the Scriptures cannot be peripheral."[4]

The curriculum is to be *life-related* in the sense that Bible content is to be made relevant to and become a part of the learners' experiences by means of the teaching ministry of the Holy Spirit, in which He illumines their minds and hearts and applies the Word to them. Bible teaching should be concerned with helping others know and obey God's Word, to learn and live Bible truths, to know and love the Lord Jesus Christ personally and deeply.

Both Bible content and student experience are to be given proper consideration in Christian education materials and programs.

The following are a number of Scripture verses that emphasize the place of biblical content (italics added):

How can a young man keep his way pure? By living according to your *Word.* (Ps. 119:9)

I have hidden your *Word* in my heart that I might not sin against you. (119:11)

Your *Word* is a lamp to my feet and a light for my path. (119:105).

He preached the *Word* to them. (Mark 2:2)

Simon Peter answered Him, "Lord, to whom shall we go? You have the *words* of eternal life." (John 6:68)

Don't you believe that I am in the Father, and that the Father is in Me? The *words* I say to you are not just My own. Rather, it is the Father, living in Me, who is doing His work. (John 14:10)

You are already clean because of the *Word* I have spoken to you. (15:3)

Your *Word* is truth. (17:17)

If you point these things out to the brothers, you will be a good minister of Christ Jesus, brought up in the *truths* of the faith and of the good *teaching* that you have followed. (1 Tim. 4:6)

He must hold firmly to the trustworthy *message* as it has been taught, so that he can encourage others by sound *doctrine* and refute those who oppose it. (Titus 1:9)

The following verses emphasize the place of Christian experience ("observe," "practice," "do," "obey," and similar words occur in many of these verses; italics are added):

For Ezra had devoted himself to the study and *observance* of the Law of the LORD, and to teaching its decrees and laws in Israel. (Ezra 7:10)

Anyone who breaks one of the least of these commandments and teaches others to do the same will be called least in the kingdom of heaven, but whoever *practices* and teaches these commands will be called great in the kingdom of heaven. (Matt. 5:19)

Go and make disciples . . . teaching them to *obey* everything I have commanded you. (28:19–20)

If any one chooses to *do* God's will, he will find out whether my teaching comes from God or whether I speak on my own. (John 7:17).

Now that you know these things, you will be blessed if you *do* them. (13:17)

You are my friends if you *do* what I command. (15:14)

Whatever you have learned or received or heard from me, or seen in me—put it into *practice.* And the God of peace will be with you. (Phil. 4:9)

Do not merely listen to the Word, and so deceive yourselves. *Do* what it says. Anyone who listens to the Word but does not *do* what it says is like a man who looks at his face in a mirror and, after looking at himself, goes away and immediately forgets what he looks like. But the man who looks intently into the perfect Law that gives freedom, and continues to do this, not forgetting what he has heard, but *doing* it—he will be blessed in what he *does.* (James 1:22–25)

Anyone, then, who knows the good he ought to *do* and doesn't *do* it, sins. (4:17)

The Holy Spirit is related to the Bible in that Bible content is inspired by Him, should be taught under His guidance, and is to be communicated to students through teachers working in cooperation with Him.

Neoorthodox Christian educators advocate a "gospel-centered" curriculum. According to D. Campbell Wyckoff, the curriculum should center in "the Gospel of God's redeeming activity in Jesus Christ,"[5] not in Christ, the Bible, the students, or the church. Sara Little takes the same view: "Such a curriculum centers more on the message and purpose of the Bible than the exact text,"[6] which she believes contains errors. Manuel Flores agrees with this position when he suggests that Christian teachers should teach not the Bible but the message of the Bible.[7] According to this concept the content of Christian education is God's *acts* of revelation and the *meaning of* those acts.

This view is defective for three reasons.

First, it is guilty of reading into the word "gospel." It destroys the clear biblical teaching that the Good News is God's plan of salvation from sin by His grace, through faith in Christ (1 Cor. 15:1–3). This neoorthodox view makes the gospel mean something other than the outworking of God's whole redemptive plan. To a neoorthodox person, the gospel is God's present acts, in which He reveals Himself directly to individuals in subjective existential encounter, through a fallible Bible.

Second, it makes man the authority over the Bible, rather than vice versa, since the Bible reader must determine what in the Bible points to God's "message" and what does not.

Third, it waters down biblical content. According to neoorthodoxy the Bible "message" is more important than the Bible "text" because the text contains errors. But if the text is unreliable, how can its *message* be reliable? If God cannot produce an infallible Book, errorless in its original writings, then how can people have confidence that the message of God's Book is any more reliable than the text?[8]

MULL IT OVER

1. Why should we be concerned about teaching the facts of the Bible?
2. What problems may arise if we are concerned only with imparting Bible facts?
3. In your Bible teaching are you stressing both scriptural content and its life relevance? Evaluate a recent lesson or two and ask yourself, Am I giving adequate emphasis to both?

CHAPTER 10
THE HOLY SPIRIT AND
BIBLICAL INTERPRETATION

Have you ever sat in a living-room Bible study group and given your view on a verse—and then another person in the group commented that the verse means something entirely different? And both of you claim you were taught by the Holy Spirit!

If the Holy Spirit is the Interpreter of Scripture, how can people hold opposing views on some scriptural passages or issues, and which view is valid? If a person senses the work of the Holy Spirit in his heart, does that mean he automatically knows the correct view of a Bible verse? If the Spirit interprets the Word privately to individual believers, how can one determine the correct view among several conflicting interpretations?

The blessed Spirit is not only the true Author of the written Word but also its supreme and true Expositor—H.C.G. Moule[1]

This fact, however, raises a number of thorny questions. If human interpretations confuse the clarity of the Word, is the Bible no longer authoritative? Is a person inconsistent if he allows the right of private judgment and at the same time claims that his interpretations are right and another's wrong?

Is the Bible unclear in its meanings? Can only a select few have insight into the meaning of Scripture? Are the "deep things of God" and His "thoughts" (1 Cor. 2:10–11) understood only by some Christians? Can a

Christian claim infallibility for his interpretation of a Bible passage simply on the claim that the Holy Spirit "taught" him that meaning?

In what sense does the Holy Spirit give insight into the Bible's meaning? Does such "light" come suddenly? Or is it the result of study? If it is the latter, can the Bible's meaning be ascertained by rational processes apart from the Holy Spirit?

How does the Spirit's role in interpretation relate to His work in illumination? Are they the same? If not, how do they differ?

These are vital issues because, as Joseph Parker explained, "there is no function assigned to the Spirit more important for us to understand than that by which He assures to the church a profound and correct interpretation of Scripture."[2] Eternal truth must be understood and correctly interpreted.

Hermeneutics, the science and art of biblical interpretation, is of primary concern to evangelicals because of their commitment to the inerrancy and authority of the Bible. The task of Bible interpreters is to seek to ascertain the meaning of Bible passages to their original hearers and readers and to determine how that meaning relates to readers today.[3] Biblical scholars have wrestled and are wrestling with serious hermeneutical issues, but comparatively little attention has been given to the Holy Spirit's role in hermeneutics.

Since inaccurate interpretation of Scripture can lead to improper conduct, one must be sure he is interpreting properly. Adequate application of truth builds on an adequate understanding of truth. A distorted meaning of a Bible verse or passage may result in misguided living.

If a teacher wishes to guide his students into a proper understanding of Scripture as a basis for a growing spiritual life, he must be involved in hermeneutics, in the process of seeking to ascertain the meaning of the Bible's statements, commands, and questions. This means, as already suggested in this book, that the interpreters (teachers and students alike) must depend on the Holy Spirit "to guide and direct"[4] them in their involvement in the interpretive process. But what does that guidance mean? And what does it imply? Fourteen propositions are suggested as a means of addressing some of these issues.

1. The Spirit's ministry in Bible interpretation does not mean He gives

new revelation. His work is always through and in association with the written Word of God, not beyond it or in addition to it.

2. The role of the Spirit in interpreting the Bible does not mean that one's interpretations are infallible. Inerrancy and hence infallibility are characteristics of the Bible's original manuscripts, but not of the Bible's interpreters. The manuscripts were inerrant because the Holy Spirit guarded and guided the writers to record what He wanted recorded, word for word. But such a superintending work cannot be claimed for interpreters of the Word. In inspiration the Holy Spirit superintended the authors to override any human error. In interpretation the Holy Spirit guides, but He does not guard against infallibility. To elevate one's interpretations to the level of infallibility would blur the distinctions between inspiration (a past, now completed work of the Spirit in the recording of Scripture) and interpretation (a present, ongoing work of the Spirit in helping interpreters comprehend Scripture). Also it would ascribe to Protestants a level of infallibility for human leaders that evangelicals reject in Roman Catholicism.

Therefore allowing the right of private (individual) judgment in interpreting the Bible does not mean that all the results of private interpretation are accurate.

3. The work of the Spirit in interpretation does not mean that He gives some interpreters a mental sharpness for seeing truths under the surface that are not evident to other dedicated Bible students. The interpreter, then, if he thinks he finds a "hidden" meaning divergent from the normal, literal meaning of the passage, cannot claim the Holy Spirit's help.

4. The role of the Holy Spirit in Bible interpretation means that the unregenerate do not welcome and apply God's truth, though they are able to intellectually comprehend many of its statements.

5. The Spirit's role in hermeneutics does not mean that only Bible scholars can understand the Bible. The Bible was given to be understood by all; hence its interpretation is not in the hands of an elite few. (See the comments on 1 John 2:20, 27 in chapter 4.) And yet believers ought not neglect the interpretive helps that can be afforded by biblical scholars.

6. The Holy Spirit's role in interpreting Scripture requires spiritual devotion on the part of the interpreter. According to Bernard Ramm, "Thomas

Aquinas used to pray and fast when he came to a difficult passage of Scripture. Most of the scholars whose biblical studies have blessed the church have mixed prayers generously with their studies."[5] "A deep religious experience has enlightened many an otherwise ill-instructed mind as to the meaning of much of Holy Writ."[6] "Apart from the quickening of the Spirit, the interpreter will have only words and phrases. Only through the Holy Spirit can he enter into the meaning of the biblical writers."[7]

However, this is not to say that prayer automatically guarantees that a person's interpretations will be accurate. Spiritual devotion, depth, and sensitivity make correct interpretations more *possible* but do not assure their accuracy. More is involved, as other propositions indicate.

7. The Holy Spirit's work in interpretation means that lack of spiritual preparedness hinders accurate interpretation.[8] A Christian who is not obeying the truth and is not yielded to the Lord is unable to understand the Word (1 Cor. 3:1–3) and "is not acquainted with the teaching about righteousness" (Heb. 5:13). A Christian who is living in sin is susceptible to making inaccurate Bible interpretations because his mind and heart are not in harmony with the Spirit. As Chafer wrote, "Carnality of life excludes [believers] from understanding, or progressing in, the deep things of God."[9] God reveals His truths by the Spirit only to spiritual Christians. "The spiritual man" has greater depth in his discernment of spiritual truths (1 Cor. 2:15) than a "worldly" Christian.

8. The role of the Spirit in interpretation is no substitute for diligent study. With a heart sensitive to the Spirit, the interpreter must study the Word intensely. The point here is that the Spirit does not make study superfluous. "The more self-consciously active the interpreter is in the process, the more likely is the Spirit's illumination."[10] The Holy Spirit works through the efforts of the individual as he reads the Bible, studies it, meditates on it, and consults other works about it. In the inspiration of the Bible the Holy Spirit was working, but so were the human authors. In a similar way, human work is involved in the interpretation of the Bible.

9. The Spirit's work in biblical interpretation does not rule out the use of study helps such as Bible commentaries, study helps, dictionaries, encyclopedias, and concordances. "It is often asserted by devout people that they can know the Bible competently without helps."[11] They assume they

can go to the Bible and the Holy Spirit interprets it for them directly. This seems to them more spiritual than relying on man's writings. Ramm answers this view by stating that no one has "either the right or the learning to bypass all the godly learning"[12] of other Bible scholars both past and present. He suggests that such an affirmation is "a veiled egotism."[13]

Of course commentaries can come between a person and the Bible. It is possible to rely on others' interpretations and neglect one's own personal study of the Scriptures. Rather than using commentaries and other study helps as a crutch and accepting unquestioningly others' views, one should consult them and evaluate the views suggested in light of his own study of the Scriptures (Acts 17:11). This should be done prayerfully and humbly in dependence on the Spirit's guidance. Chafer addresses this point well: "No student of the Scripture should be satisfied to traffic only in the results of the study of other men. The field is inexhaustible and its treasures ever new. No worthy astronomer limits his attention to the findings of other men, but is himself ever gazing into the heavens both to verify and to discover; and no worthy theologian will be satisfied alone with the result of the research of other theologians, but will himself be ever searching the Scriptures."[14]

10. The ministry of the Holy Spirit in Bible interpretation does not mean interpreters can ignore common sense and logic. Since the Spirit is "the Spirit of truth" (John 14:17; 15:26; 16:13), He would not teach concepts that fail to meet the tests of truth. (In a correspondence theory of truth, truth is what corresponds to the actual state of affairs.)[15] The Holy Spirit does not guide into interpretations that contradict each other or fail to have logical, internal consistency.

Two believers may be spiritual, but one or both may be wrong in their understanding of a Bible passage because of failure to think through the Bible logically. Two contradictory views may both be wrong, or one may be wrong, but they cannot both be correct. The Spirit seeks to aid the Spirit-filled learner to think clearly and accurately. The interpreter "must employ principles of reasoning in making inductions, deductions, analogies, and comparisons."[16]

Bible students recognize that while the Bible is a unique book—inspired by the Holy Spirit and therefore infallible and authoritative—it is a written means of communication (from God to man), which suggests that it must be understood in that light. As with any written communication, the interpreter seeks to expose the meaning of the passage in its original setting, as it was understood by its original hearers. The Bible was written in languages unknown to most modern readers, in cultural environments that differ from Western culture, in geographical settings that are distant from most present-day Bible readers, and in literary styles unlike many common literary forms today. These gaps—linguistic, cultural, geographical, and literary—are often hindrances to communication. Removing these hindrances or closing the gaps is a vital part of properly interpreting the Bible.[17]

Just as one uses common sense in seeking to bridge communication gaps within his own culture, so he should use common sense in interpreting the Bible. A reader normally gives an author the benefit of the doubt if the author makes a statement that seemingly conflicts with a previous statement. The same should be granted the Bible. Also a reader normally uses principles of logic in seeking to understand an author's writing. He does not read into the writing a meaning that is foreign to the material. The same should be granted with regard to the Bible.

Though spiritual truths often supersede man's reasoning ability, they do not contradict or conflict with reason. Clear thinking, then, along with normal procedures followed in comprehending written communications, is essential in Bible interpretation and harmonizes with the Holy Spirit's role.

11. The place of the Holy Spirit in interpreting the Bible means that He does not normally give sudden intuitive flashes of insight into the meaning of Scripture. Though many passages are readily understood, the meaning of others may come to light only gradually in the arduous process of careful study (as stated earlier in proposition 8). Still other times a Bible student may concentrate on a passage a long time with its meaning still eluding him. But later, after leaving the passage for awhile, the meaning may seem to jump to his mind suddenly. "The interpreter's struggle to understand always precedes that . . . experience, it does not occur in connection with a text on which one has expended no effort."[18] This sudden insight, if it occurs, does not come apart from his having studied the passage earlier.

To speak of the Spirit's part in hermeneutics is not to suggest some mysterious work that is beyond verification or validation. James Lee argues against the view that the role of the Holy Spirit in interpretation and religious instruction means that His activity is a "mysterious and unfathomable" work[19] so that teaching-learning activity is unexplainable, unpredictable, or unverifiable,[20] or that teaching and learning are "miracles magically wrought by . . . zaps of the Holy Spirit."[21] Though Lee correctly stresses that learning does not come by sudden impulses of the Holy Spirit, he then goes too far by ruling out the Holy Spirit's work altogether.[22] To depend on the Holy Spirit, Lee says, is to "spookify" religious instruction as if it were "an ethereal, mysterious, nonterrestrial affair which is fundamentally beyond the regular workings of nature."[23] But while some educators may seek to overemphasize the Holy Spirit, an equally dangerous direction is to neglect His work completely.

12. The Spirit's ministry in interpreting the Bible is included in but is not identical with illumination. Illumination, as discussed in chapter 4, is the Spirit's work on the minds and hearts of believers that enables them not only to discern the truth but also to receive, welcome, and apply it. In interpretation a believer is aided by the Spirit *to ascertain* the meaning of a passage. This is the first step in illumination. But illumination is not complete until one has applied it to his life. Interpretation involves *perception;* illumination includes interpretation, but it also involves *reception.*

13. The role of the Spirit in scriptural interpretation does not mean that all parts of the Bible are equally clear in meaning. Some scholars claim that all the Bible is equally perspicuous, that its meaning is clear and plain. However, perspicuity does not mean that all parts of the Bible are equally clear. Even Peter said that Paul's epistles "contain some things that are hard to understand" (2 Pet. 3:16). Perspicuity means instead that the central message of the Bible, the message of salvation, is clear to all. Of course, as discussed in chapter 3, unsaved people may not welcome the plan of salvation, though they have understood it mentally.

14. The Spirit's work in interpretation does not result in believers having a comprehensive and completely accurate understanding of the entire Scriptures. The exact meaning of many passages still eludes many Bible scholars, even after lifetime study in the Scriptures. The precise meaning of some verses cannot be known until we see the Savior "face to face" (1 Cor. 13:12). Students of the Bible,

even though they are devout and are Spirit-taught, must admit that the correct interpretation of at least some passages simply cannot be fully ascertained this side of heaven.

These propositions suggest that these elements are necessary for properly interpreting the Bible: salvation, spiritual maturity, diligent study, common sense and logic, and humble dependence on the Spirit of God for discernment. Clearly the Holy Spirit is very much involved in the process of a believer's interpretation of the Bible. Teachers can help guide their students in these directions as they seek to help them comprehend the Bible as an important step in spiritual growth.

POINTS TO PONDER

1. Suppose someone says to you, "The Holy Spirit taught me that this Bible passage means this," but another person senses from the Holy Spirit that it means something else. How would you go about determining which view, if either of them, is correct?
2. Does the Holy Spirit's teaching ministry mean you can have special insight into supposed "hidden" meanings in the Bible that others don't have? Why or why not?
3. If we rely on the Holy Spirit as our Teacher, why should we spend time studying the Bible? What place should commentaries and other study helps have in our lesson preparation?
4. Do you agree or disagree with the view that depending on the Holy Spirit makes religious instruction "an ethereal or mysterious, nonterrestrial affair"? Why?

PART FOUR
THE HOLY SPIRIT IN
THE TEACHING-LEARNING PROCESS

The Holy Spirit's teaching ministry is needed in relation to the content and to the teacher. It is also needed in relation to the process in which teachers teach and learners learn. Unless God's Spirit is operating in the teaching and learning activities, the educational process is not Christian. It is important to see how the Holy Spirit operates in or is related to these four aspects of the teaching-learning process: the goal of Christian teaching, the nature of learning, the principles of effective learning and teaching, and the use of methods and materials.

But this immediately raises a problem: Do principles of pedagogy conflict with the work of the Holy Spirit? If the Holy Spirit is ministering to pupils through dedicated teachers, why consider the principles of teaching and learning? Benson replies:

> Is not the Holy Spirit dishonored by the teacher who seeks to be guided by the laws of pedagogy? Not at all. One does not dishonor the Holy Spirit by complying with the laws of gravitation. One does not dishonor the Holy Spirit in becoming acquainted with the laws which govern the working of the human mind. No one was more fully led by the Holy Spirit than our Lord Jesus Christ and yet no one more consistently observed the laws of pedagogy.[1]

CHAPTER 11
PRINCIPLES OF LEARNING AND
THE WORK OF THE HOLY SPIRIT

THE GOAL OF CHRISTIAN EDUCATION

A clear understanding of the goal or aim of Christian education is basic to effective teaching. In fact anyone who seeks success in any endeavor must have a clear and definite aim. However, if God does the work, does the worker need to be concerned about aims? The answer to this question is suggested by Eavey, who states that "teaching that lacks aim is poor teaching, even if it is characterized by the presence of many good qualities."[1]

Christian education has frequently been hampered not only by aimlessness or lack of clarity but also by improper or inadequate aims. When asked, "What is the purpose of Christian teaching?" many teachers reply, "To teach the Bible." But this is inadequate as the *ultimate* goal.

Of course, Christian teaching involves teaching Bible facts. In a sense it *is* true that the goal is "to teach the Bible" because, as we saw in chapter 9, the Bible is the essential body of content to be transmitted. *But knowledge of doctrinal and spiritual truths falls short of the ultimate goal of Christian education for three reasons.*

First, knowledge is worth little unless it can be applied and used in fruitful ways.

Second, knowing what is in the Bible does not guarantee that the one who possesses that knowledge will love it, obey it, and apply it to life. Many individuals can quote memory verses but fail to live them. The Pharisees of Jesus' day knew the Scriptures, and many unbelievers today have mastered Bible content but have been unchanged by its truths.

Third, Bible knowledge is but a means to an end, not an end in itself. Bible knowledge is a means of fostering spiritual growth, but it does not always guarantee it. As I have stated elsewhere, "Theoretical knowledge of the content of the Bible, while absolutely indispensable, does not in itself automatically guarantee spiritual development. More is needed—a responsive heart with a willingness to appropriate the truths of the Scriptures into one's own experience."[2] Therefore the goal of Christian teaching, while it certainly includes the communication of Bible facts, must extend beyond that.

Most Christian educators concur that the one inclusive and ultimate aim of Christian teaching is "that the man of God may be thoroughly equipped for every good work" (2 Tim. 3:17). The words "thoroughly equipped" translate two Greek words (*artios* and *exērtismenos*) that are close in meaning. The NASB renders these two words "adequate" and "equipped." The first word means "in fit shape or condition" and the second means "altogether fit."[3] Each word occurs only here in the New Testament. Helping believers be adequately equipped for living to God's glory is the major purpose for which the Scriptures were given. All Christian teaching should be directed to the one final aim of building up those taught so that they develop in character. Teaching is not merely giving out information; it involves guiding others into finding the truth for themselves.

Murch defines the aim as "fitting men to live in perfect harmony with the will of God."[4] Christian education is intended to help others "become mature," to help them come ever closer to "the whole measure of the fullness of Christ" (Eph. 4:13). Paul expressed the goal of teaching this way: "Admonishing and teaching everyone with all wisdom, so that we may present everyone perfect [mature] in Christ" (Col. 1:28).

Spiritual maturity means *knowing* God personally (not simply knowing about Him) and *loving* Him (not simply learning of Him) with all one's heart, soul, mind, and strength (Mark 12:30). Henry Blackaby and Claude King emphasize this love relationship the Lord wants us to have with Him.[5] Spiritual maturity means being filled with the Holy Spirit and yielded to Christ (Rom. 6:13). It means having one's life Christ-controlled. It means letting Christ be the center of one's life, influencing, penetrating, and directing every area. Thus Christianity is not one among many "compartments" of life; instead, it is to permeate all of life. The spiritually mature Christian is the one who follows Solomon's words, "In *all* your ways acknowledge Him" (Prov. 3:6, italics added).

Spiritual depth is measured not by the extent of one's knowledge of the Scriptures but by the consistency of one's "walk" (conduct) in accord with God's standards. In that way a believer's walk pleases God (Rom. 13:13; Gal. 5:16–25; Eph. 4:1; 5:2, 8; Phil. 3:16; Col. 1:10; 2:6; 4:5; 1 Thess. 2:12; 1 John 1:7; 2:6; 2 John 6; 3 John 4). This view of teaching (instructing others in content whereby they are encouraged to develop spiritually) is reinforced by a study of the Hebrew and Greek words for "teach," "explain," "instruct," "disciple," and "train." Several sources may be consulted for information on the interesting shades of meaning in these words.[6]

Several specific aspects of this ultimate goal of spiritual maturity include helping others (a) increase in knowledge, (b) improve in attitudes, (c) grow in appreciation, and (d) develop in skills. Teaching is helping students gain more information, new understandings, new insights, changed attitudes, new points of view, new skills, deeper values.

Robert Mager has written several excellent books that emphasize teaching aims that go beyond the intellectual assimilation of facts.[7] LeRoy Ford speaks of learning outcomes in four areas: knowledge, insight, attitude, skill.[8] The first two are cognitive objectives, the other two, affective. Others have suggested five affective objectives, in this ascending order:

- *receiving* (becoming aware of a phenomenon or value or fact, becoming willing to tolerate or receive it, giving controlled or selective attention to it),
- *responding* (complying to a phenomenon or value or fact, becoming willing to respond to it, being satisfied with or enjoying the response),
- *valuing* (accepting a value, preferring it, committing oneself to it),
- *organizing* (conceptualizing a value, organizing one's values into a value system),
- *characterizing* (becoming oriented to a way of life or predisposed to act in a certain way, being characterized internally by a set of values and attitudes).[9]

LeBar mentions several comprehensive objectives for Christian education: "Right relation to God the Father, Son, the Holy Spirit; knowledge and love and practical use of the Bible; formulation of a Christian world and life view; a progressively closer walk with Christ; assuming of responsibility in the church, for the lost everywhere, and in the civic community."[10]

Christian teaching is concerned with spiritual transformation. Therefore we should be content with nothing less than spiritual change, with Christ-honoring results in every area of our students' lives. We should teach in such a way that those under our charge come to accept Christ as their personal Savior and walk with Him, grow in Him, know Him, serve Him, obey Him, worship Him, and enjoy Him.

An effective teacher cannot be satisfied with "how well the lesson went" or "how much information I got across." Instead, to see lives changed is the most significant commitment a teacher can make.—Dennis H. Dirks[11]

Obviously one cannot accomplish these purposes apart from the empowering and guiding ministry of the Holy Spirit. Christian teachers recognize with Paul their insufficiencies and dependence on God: "Not that we are competent to claim anything for ourselves, but our competence comes from God" (2 Cor. 3:5). As Christ said, "Apart from Me, you can do nothing" (John 15:5).

According to neoorthodoxy, the goal of teaching is different. It is to help students prepare for and experience encounter or confrontation directly with God,[12] in which the Bible *becomes* the Word of God. A basic error in the neoorthodox view of the teaching-learning process is the concept that this process is revelational. I discussed this elsewhere: "Of course, learning, in the broad sense, is revelational in that new truths, skills, or attitudes are made known or 'revealed.' But the teaching and learning of the Bible should be thought of as an illuminational process, not revelational. In other words, learning and appropriating the truths of God to one's life is not an act in which the Bible *becomes* revelatory; instead it is an act by which the Holy Spirit illuminates the heart in respect to that which *already is* a written revelation of and from God. Learning the facts of the Bible and having one's life changed by them is the Spirit's work of illumination, not revelation."[13]

WHAT IS LEARNING?

Because spiritual growth or Christian maturity is the goal of Christian education, all Christian teaching must be directed toward helping students learn and grow in the Christian life. In view of the fact that teaching is helping people learn, "the basic problem is not teaching, but learning."[14] Unless teachers discover how people learn, they will not be able to teach as they ought. The test of real teaching is real learning. This is why Thom and Joani Schultz urge teachers to "focus on learning rather than teaching."[15]

Vieth stresses knowing the nature of learning: "A worker in wood conforms to the laws of the material he is working with in order to produce the smoothness of surface, strength, shade of stain, and other qualities in his finished product. A worker with human beings is but using refined common sense when he complies with the laws of growth with which God has endowed his 'material' in order to produce the highest quality of Christian character."[16]

In view of the goal of teaching previously discussed, learning is more than listening, reciting, or memorizing. Students have not necessarily learned if they have only a mental apprehension of truth without actually experiencing it, appropriated to their lives by the Holy Spirit. Facts not perceived, skills taught in isolation, and verbalisms presented to passive, unmotivated students fail to effect genuine spiritual growth. Learning is the process in which a person modifies his or her behavior, by the Spirit's power, to conform more to the will of God and the image of Christ. Vieth writes: "True learning is an inward experience through which the pupil appropriates to his own life and character the new knowledge, insight, attitude, or skill in living which may be mediated to him by the educational process. He is like a tree which puts forth its leaves, blossoms, and fruit because of the inner life which is flowing through it, and not like a Christmas tree, to which others fix tinsel, shiny balls, and lights which are not really its own and never will be."[17]

The Greek word for "learn" *(manthanō)* sometimes means to acquire information or knowledge about something or someone. Other times it means to "appropriate to oneself less through instruction than through experience or practice."[18] The former is indicated in Matthew 24:32, where

115

the Lord told His disciples to "learn" a parable. He also urged others to "learn" from Him (11:29). Paul exhorted Timothy to continue in what he had "learned" (2 Tim. 3:14). And the Romans were to avoid those who taught doctrines contrary to the truths they had "learned" (Rom. 16:17). *Manthanō* is also used in this way in other passages (Mark 13:28; John 6:45; 7:15; 1 Cor. 4:6; 14:31, 35; Eph. 4:20; Phil. 4:9; Col. 1:7; 1 Tim. 2:11; 2 Tim. 3:7; Rev. 14:3). The second meaning, appropriation through experience, is used five times (Phil. 4:11, "I have learned to be content"; 1 Tim. 5:4, children should "learn . . . to put their religion into practice"; 1 Tim. 5:13, younger widows sometimes "learn to be idle" [NASB]; Titus 3:14, believers "must learn to devote themselves to doing what is good"; Heb. 5:8, Christ "learned obedience from what He suffered").

Theories of how people learn differ. Perhaps the theory of learning that best matches what is seen in the Scriptures and that best explains the phenomenon of learning is a theory that combines the best of several views, that is, an eclectic theory. Several writers suggest this approach.[19]

Students learn best when teachers have established conditions favorable to the working of the Holy Spirit.

As individuals recognize their needs and submit to the teaching of the Holy Spirit in meeting those needs, learning takes place. The Holy Spirit is essential in learning God's truth, for people can learn nothing of spiritual significance unless they are God-taught. Students have not fully learned until the Holy Spirit has made the truths of God relevant to their life-needs.

PRINCIPLES OF LEARNING

What facilitates learning? What factors or conditions are necessary for effective learning? How do pupils best learn? How can teachers cooperate with the Holy Spirit's "laws" that govern good learning?

People learn best when they are motivated, when the subject matter is relevant to them, when they are actively involved, and when they are ready to learn.

THE PRINCIPLE OF MOTIVATION

One key factor in the process of learning, and perhaps its basic principle, is motivation. If a student has no motivation, he will experience little or no learning. If two individuals are equally capable of learning, and one learns and the other does not, it is evident that the one who learned wanted to learn or was motivated to learn, whereas the other was not.

Motivating learning simply means making learning desirable or desired. It is causing people to want to learn. It is important that we understand this principle so we can use proper motivational factors and lead our students to want to learn, rather than coercing them to learn.

Motivation facilitates learning. When people are motivated to learn, they learn more quickly and the results are more lasting. The stronger the motivation, the more rapid and effective the learning.

Motivation is integrally related to interests and needs. Students' needs or innate drives, placed within them by the Lord Himself, prompt actions. People learn best when they are interested and sense personal needs. This suggests that we, with the aid of the Holy Spirit, should seek to discover students' needs, relate those needs to the Word of God, and thus enjoy the results of seeing motivated pupils learn. Sometimes learners sense their needs and are already motivated to learn. Other times teachers must make them aware of their needs before they are motivated to learn. A sense of need is the starting point of all learning.

There are two kinds of motivation: extrinsic and intrinsic. Extrinsic motivation with its prizes or rewards is not the most desirable kind of motivation because it suggests that the spiritual life is not worth seeking for its own sake. It implies that the Bible material to be studied is not important enough to study for its own worth. Extrinsic incentives often create only temporary motivation and do not always cause students to give their best to their study.

In contrast, intrinsic motivation taps students' inner drives and urges and leads them to what is worth knowing and doing for its own sake. This is the kind of motivation the Holy Spirit seeks to generate in the lives of others.

The approval of the teacher, and more especially of the class, affords a better motive than prizes. The inner sense of satisfaction from duty well done is a better motive than approval of teacher and class. The inner joy of having pleased the Master is the highest of all motives and should be appealed to whenever possible.[20]

The believer's chief intrinsic motive is, or should be, to conform to the desires of the One who redeemed him.

How does the Holy Spirit relate to the matter of motivation? How does He motivate, if at all? The Spirit of God does several things with reference to student motivation.

1. He seeks to create in the students an awareness of their needs. He endeavors to help them sense their own personal weaknesses. This He can do for them only as they are open to His convincing and teaching ministries, through their study of the written Word, prayer, and meditation.

2. He seeks to lead individuals to Christ and His Word for answers to their needs. He is waiting to supply all their needs according to God's glorious riches in Christ Jesus (Phil. 4:19).

3. The Holy Spirit seeks to use teachers in leading students to the highest motives. Teachers should cultivate an appreciation for the loftiest motives, so that students' deepest needs are met through the teaching of the Word.

4. The Holy Spirit seeks to give spiritual orientation to the inner drives and urges of human nature. Humans desire and need approval, new experiences, achievement, and expression. Each of these has the potential for fulfillment in the spiritual realm. For example, students want approval. But, of course, they ought to be more motivated by approval from the Lord than by approval from parents, teachers, or friends. "We obey His commands and do what pleases *Him*" (1 John 3:22, italics added). "A man's ways" are to be "pleasing to the LORD" (Prov. 16:7, italics added). The desire for new experiences should motivate students to seek the new joys of deeper godly living, through the strength of the Spirit. The need for achievement can be met by encouraging students to develop ideals and reach specific goals in Christian service and living. The need for activity or expression challenges others to diligent service for the Lord in the local church and elsewhere.

5. The Holy Spirit also grants Christian teachers insight during lesson preparation to make them aware of student needs, and insight during lesson presentation to help them make students aware of their own needs.

6. The Holy Spirit seeks to motivate students to learn by upholding before them ideals and goals in Christian living and service. The wise Christian teacher motivates learning by instilling ideals of conduct and by encouraging students to work toward significant goals. The New Testament contains numerous exhortations to Christians to achieve various spiritual goals (for example, Phil. 2:12–14; Col. 3:1–2, 5–17; Heb. 6:1; 2 Pet. 1:5–7; 3:18).

Spirit-directed learning is the highest form of intrinsic motivation. In learning and applying divine truth, no motive can substitute for the pure inner urges implanted by God's Spirit. Believers who are filled with the Spirit desire to do "the will of God from [the] heart" (Eph. 6:6). They desire to "devote themselves to doing what is good" (Titus 3:14), to "set [their] hearts on things above" (Col. 3:1), and to "do . . . all in the name of the Lord Jesus" (3:17).

Of course, only people who have been regenerated by God's Spirit through faith in Christ can enjoy full motivation for Christian living. Salvation brings "new motivation which will be the power for breaking old habits and forming new ones."[21] Conversion, Edge points out, provides "the only adequate foundation and motivation for Christian living."[22]

The unsaved student has little or no motivation for learning spiritual truth, until the Holy Spirit moves within his heart to convince him of sin and of his need of the Savior. At that point, the one motivating factor present is the desire for eternal life, acceptance with God, and a solution to personal sin. At salvation, a person becomes "a new creation" in Jesus Christ (2 Cor. 5:17) with a new set of values and motives, waiting to be tapped and channeled by Spirit-led Christian teachers. Without Spirit-guided motivation, there is little or no interest on the part of students. And if they have little interest, there is little or no Spirit-directed learning.

THE PRINCIPLE OF RELEVANCE

Relevance to life-needs is the second principle that governs effective learning. Students must not only be motivated to learn; they must see how the truth relates to them personally.

Students learn to the extent that lessons relate to their personal needs or problems. This principle is similar to, if not the same as, what some educators call the law of satisfaction. When spiritual needs are met, student interest is increased, learning is enhanced, and satisfaction results. "Learning occurs because a need is satisfied either directly or indirectly."[23] And Howard Mayes and James Long affirm that "people are more receptive to life-related Bible teaching" than to teaching that does not relate to life needs.[24] Felt needs are the "doorway to involvement."[25]

The apostle Paul was a master at relating truth to people's needs. His epistles ring with relevance, and he addressed various problems head-on.[26]

This principle of learning suggests to Christian teachers that they depend on the Spirit of God to enable them to (1) introduce their lessons in ways that will capture interest and that will relate to student problems, needs, and experiences—as Christ often did; (2) show how the Bible is relevant to learners' experiences; and (3) lead students to see and appropriate the Word of the Lord as the answer to their personal needs.

LeBar summarizes this important principle of learning: "If our pupils see no connection between their own needs and the Word, it may be spoken into the air in their vicinity, but will yield little fruit because it doesn't get inside. If it is associated with an interest, they will listen with attention which may lead to something deeper. If they see how the Bible meets a need, they will make some effort to find God's answer."[27]

As Richards has stated, "People learn best when they see results in their lives."[28] And as Gangel has written, "Learning unrelated to life is as dead as faith without works."[29]

THE PRINCIPLE OF ACTIVITY

The third principle of learning is also called the law of experience, practice, involvement, or interaction.

People learn by doing. The activity may be physical, mental, or emotional, but there must be activity if learning is to take place.

Too often, Sunday-school classes and other class settings in churches and schools treat students as if they are passive learners. They are not given opportunity to be actively engaged in the learning process. Teachers assume that if students are quiet, they are learning. But that is not necessarily the case.

Mayes and Long offer interesting and practical suggestions on how to involve students in the classroom.[30] And the Schultzes suggest ways to engage children and young people in what they call "active learning" and "interactive learning."[31] As I wrote elsewhere, "By means of activities, assignments, and projects students have opportunity to reinforce what is learned in the classroom, put into practice the truths taught, internalize the concepts studied, and develop initiative and responsibility."[32]

But how can learning be an active process if learning depends on the Holy Spirit? Doesn't the Spirit's presence in the learning process suggest that students need to rely only on Him, rather than on their participation or personal involvement? The answer to the second question is negative, because one thing the Spirit purposes to do in the learning process is to help students interact with what they have discovered in the Word so they become more Christlike in their attitudes and actions. The Holy Spirit encourages pupil activity so that there will be interaction of the total personality—mind, emotion, and will—with God's Word. And He guides submissive teachers to assist their learners in interacting with the right persons, the right things, and the right ideas, to the end that they may advance spiritually. Spirit-filled teachers are capable of being directed by the Spirit in choosing life problems for their pupils to deal with and issues for them to think about.

THE PRINCIPLE OF READINESS

Readiness, as a principle of learning, is related to motivation but is not identical to it. Motivation may be thought of as the stimulation of the desire to learn, whereas readiness may be thought of as the conditioning or preparedness for learning. Taken in this sense, motivation could be considered an aspect of readiness.

The principle of readiness points to the fact that *students learn more effectively when they are prepared to learn.* Readiness stimulates thinking, provides a foundation on which teachers can build, excites interest in learning, creates greater anticipation for learning, and stimulates habits of independent study.

People may be made ready to learn by various means. Activities such as reading, field trips, observation, interviews, thought questions, written assignments, and others enhance the readiness factor. Students are also ready to learn to the extent that they are conscious of their needs and are aided by proper home and teacher relationships. Other factors that affect readiness are past experiences, social pressures, physical and mental development, and awareness of spiritual deficiencies.

> Readiness also means that learning is effective to the extent that the teacher begins with the present state of the learners' knowledge and experience and seeks to guide them from the known to the unknown. If the teacher does not associate what he is teaching with his students' present experience and knowledge, the teacher may be inclined (1) to talk above the students' level of comprehension, thus making it difficult for them to understand readily what is being taught; (2) to present irrelevant and uninteresting material; and (3) to present material that is already known and therefore repetitiously boring.[33]

Meaningful learning seems to occur only when facts are woven into a meaningful fabric of related information.—Donald M. Joy[34]

Why do some students seem more eager and ready to learn than others? Several answers may be noted.

First, God has a different plan or "divine timetable" for each person. In His sovereign grace He has planned for some individuals to come to an understanding of certain truths more quickly than other students. Even in Christ's earthly ministry some were quicker to grasp His truth than others. The rate of spiritual growth for some individuals may be slower or faster at times than for others. Some students may be apathetic to learning the Bible because of sin or failure to respond to the Spirit's past teaching ministry. A Christian is grieving the Spirit if he displays lack of interest in the truth. An unregenerate person may lack enthusiasm for the things of

God simply because he is unsaved and therefore not indwelt by the Spirit (Rom. 8:9; 1 Cor. 2:14).

Second, the personalities, mental capacities, and spiritual abilities of students differ. Rate of growth varies from person to person and is determined in part by heredity and environment.

Third, teachers may be responsible for the lack of readiness on the part of some learners because of poor teacher-student relationships, ignorance of students' needs, or lack of proper adjustment to the Holy Spirit.

With reference to the principle of readiness, the Holy Spirit works through individuals' past experiences to bring them in God's own time to higher levels of spiritual living, and He conditions learners' receptivity by making them aware of existing needs. He stimulates teachers to greater personal concern for their students. And He adjusts and arranges circumstances that will help bring about learning.

This principle of learning suggests that Christian teachers should teach those spiritual truths that their students are most capable of learning at that particular stage of their spiritual development. This principle also suggests that teachers should look to the Holy Spirit to direct them in the choice of those teaching techniques that will best create student readiness. Because environment affects readiness, teachers ought to arrange environmental factors to facilitate maximum learning. This means being concerned about room appearance, furniture arrangement, room temperature, lighting, ventilation, adequate space, proper wall colors, and room "decorations" (curtains, bulletin boards, displays, etc.).

Since readiness involves the removal of hindrances to learning, it is imperative that teachers be aware of what these hindering factors are. Some factors that hinder learning are these:

- lack of motivation,
- lack of lesson preparation,
- not involving students in meaningful learning activities, and
- not relating biblical truths to life-needs.

Another factor is spiritual blindness or lack of salvation. Leading individuals to accept Christ as their Savior is the first step in giving them the readiness to comprehend Bible truths. Therefore the plan of salvation should be taught clearly and repeatedly.

Carnality or lack of yieldedness on the part of regenerate pupils also hinders learning. The main need of the Christian learner is yieldedness or commitment to the Lord. Charles Trentham states that "obedience to the truth revealed to us is a spiritual condition upon which further revelations of truth depend."[35] A believer who is living in sin is incapable of appropriating divine truth and is unable "to distinguish good from evil" (Heb. 5:14). Chafer maintains that "there can be no full or worthy apprehension of God's revealed truth by the Christian who is unspiritual or carnal. Hence the imperative aspect of a yielded life."[36] To comprehend the revelation of the mind and will of God, believers must yield their lives to God and thus have their minds transformed by the power of God to recognize "His good, pleasing, and perfect will" (Rom. 12:1–2).

Being filled with the Holy Spirit (Eph. 5:17–18) increases a believer's capacity to learn more quickly and adequately. This does not suggest, however, that a person's intelligence quotient or mental capacity is necessarily heightened by the filling of the Holy Spirit. Students are simply made more open or receptive to the Spirit's teaching ministry. The ability to learn spiritual truths increases in proportion to yieldedness to the Spirit of God. Prayer, spiritual preparation, and an obedient heart are also essential to genuine learning.

Does this emphasis, however, on learning principles and student experience nullify the work of the Spirit and suggest a return to the naturalistic educational philosophy of John Dewey and others? No, because the person who is teaching in light of these basic learning principles is really following the master Teacher, Jesus Christ—not John Dewey. Witmer addresses this fact: "Learning that takes place in life situations, that grows out of need, that is stimulated by interest, that is conceived as growth is as old as Christian education itself. The founder of Christianity Himself, the world's master Teacher, practiced that kind of education."[37]

Concern for learning principles does not take away the place of the Spirit's teaching ministry. That's because the teaching of the Holy Spirit is no substitute for learning, and learning takes place basically by means of the Holy Spirit. Therefore the prayer of each Christian should be that of the psalmist, "Give me understanding to learn your commands" (Ps. 119:73).[38]

YOUR TURN

1. Think of what you are trying to accomplish as you teach your students the Scriptures. How would you state your goals? Write down several "goal statements." How do these compare with the ideas presented in the first section of this chapter under the heading "The Goal of Christian Education"?

2. Suppose someone says to you, "Teaching has not taken place unless students learn." Would you agree or disagree with this statement? Why?

3. Since motivation is so essential to learning, can you list ways you can more effectively motivate your students to learn? What specific steps can you take in your next lesson or two?

4. Evaluate a recent lesson you have taught, asking yourself, "To what extent did I follow the principle of relevance, that is, how effectively did I relate the content to the students' needs?"

5. Think again of the lesson you evaluated as suggested in question four, and ask, "How effectively did I help prepare my pupils for the teaching-learning session? How could I have improved in this area?"

6. Can you think of any spiritual or physical factors that might hinder your students' learning?

7. How did Jesus motivate His disciples? How did He make His teaching relevant to the needs of individuals? How did He engage the disciples and others in learning activities? How did He make them ready to learn? How can you follow some of His ways of teaching in your class?

CHAPTER 12
TEACHING METHODOLOGY AND THE WORK OF THE HOLY SPIRIT

Just as certain factors facilitate learning, so certain factors govern effective teaching. Knowing the principles of teaching and how the Spirit of God works through them can greatly aid teachers in declaring truth and guiding students.

He who would gain a harvest must obey nature's laws for the growing of corn, and he who would teach a child successfully must follow the laws of teaching.—John Gregory[1]

The four principles of learning discussed in chapter 11 relate specifically to activities involving the *learner*. To learn most effectively, a person must be motivated, have his needs met, be actively involved, and be prepared.

The principles of teaching relate specifically to the self-activities of the *teacher*. Three of the more basic teaching principles are preparation, understanding of and concern for students, and communication.

THE PRINCIPLE OF PREPARATION

Effective teaching begins with a prepared teacher, as well as a prepared lesson. To teach others, Christian teachers must be in vital union with Christ, filled with the Word and the Spirit. Edge asserts that "the single most important factor that influences learning is the *life and personality* of the teacher."[2] This is true, he points out, because (1) teaching techniques are of little use unless they are used by one through whose life the truth and love of God radiate; (2) Christian truths are better understood when seen in life; (3) lives are impressed and changed more by demonstrated truths than by those merely spoken. For these reasons, Christian teachers should be selected with great care.

The apostle Paul sought to live the truths he taught. Stressing the importance of believers being Christlike, Paul urged Christians in Philippi to "join with others in following my example" and to "take note of those who live according to the pattern we gave you" (Phil. 3:17). He commended his Thessalonian converts for being "imitators" of him and "of the Lord" (1 Thess. 1:6). And he wrote to the Corinthians, "Follow my example [literally, 'become imitators of me'], as I follow the example of Christ" (1 Cor. 11:1). Paul was so consistent and exemplary in his walk before the Lord and others that he could say to the Philippians, "Whatever you have learned or received or heard from me, or seen in me put it into practice" (Phil. 4:9).

Certainly the stature of Paul's consistent spiritual life contributed immensely to the impact of his ministry.

As I have discussed elsewhere, Paul was a man of deep piety, spiritual authority, personal integrity, genuine humility, courtesy, sensitivity, fervency, tenacity, severity, serenity, felicity, and mastery.[3]

Because he was so thoroughly "prepared" spiritually he could then urge his converts to follow his Christlike example. Every Christian teacher today would do well to follow this principle of spiritual preparation exemplified by Paul. As Osberg says, unless they do so, they can hardly expect to see spiritual results from their teaching. "What difference does it make when a Christian teacher as opposed to a non-Christian teacher steps into a teaching-learning experience? Certainly the subject matter does not change. The difference lies in the teacher himself . . . [in his] value structure, attitudes, selection of curriculum, and self-disclosure to his class."[4]

The work of the Spirit in Christian education certainly does not preclude study and preparation on the part of the teachers. In fact, the better prepared the teachers are, the better the Holy Spirit can use them in class sessions.

But what about times when the Holy Spirit has seemed to use our poorly prepared teaching efforts and has apparently accomplished much? While it is true that the Spirit can and does override a teacher's bungling, lack of preparation on his part is nowhere encouraged in the Bible. A creative teacher brings to his class a prepared heart, a knowledge of his subject, a conviction of the truths to be taught, and a desire to guide his students into the spiritual experiences he has enjoyed with the Lord.

THE PRINCIPLE OF UNDERSTANDING OF AND CONCERN FOR STUDENTS

Successful teaching depends not only on knowledge of your Savior and your lessons but also on knowledge of your students. Your personal interest in and an understanding and appreciation of each student's problems and needs contribute to a close personal relationship between you and the student which, in turn, fosters learning. Several books provide helpful information on characteristics of students at various age levels.[5] Knowing the backgrounds, interests, difficulties, ambitions, concerns, frustrations, attitudes, needs, and levels of maturity of individuals enables teachers to select the most appropriate methods and teaching procedures. And this allows the Spirit to work to greatest advantage.

The more intimately you know your students, the better equipped you are to meet their needs. As you come to know and work with them as individuals, you, with the aid of the Holy Spirit, can more easily direct them to solutions found in God's Word. As Edge asks, "Does the farmer's study and understanding of the earth make God unnecessary? Not at all. It is still God's seed. It is still God's earth. It is still His sun and rain. It is still He who germinates the seed and who gives the increase. The farmer just cooperates more intelligently with God [who] enables him to bring forth a greater fruitage."[6]

Because only the Holy Spirit knows what changes must be affected in learners' hearts, it is imperative that we look to Him for greater insight into human personality and individual needs.

More than knowledge of our students is necessary, however. An effective teacher is also concerned for them. In a survey of 257 student-teacher candidates at a Christian college, "a concern for pupils" was ranked as the most admirable quality for influential teachers. Of nine clusters of admirable qualities, the "caring" cluster (which included "concern for pupils") ranked highest. Of personality factors, "patience" and "love" were the two highest in rank.[7]

THE PRINCIPLE OF COMMUNICATION

An effective teacher is one who, under the guidance of God's Spirit, communicates the truth he or she knows to the students he or she knows. Communicating God's truth implies that teachers use words understood in the same way by them and their students, and that the unknown be taught or approached through truths already known. It implies that under the Spirit's direction, every means possible and necessary be used to convey truth, such as illustrations, audio and visual aids, examinations, class participation, a permissive atmosphere, removal of distractions, and a proper teaching pace.

With regard to teaching pace or the rate at which teachers attempt to communicate quantity of content, Doll offers this suggestion: "Rather than teaching too much at a time, which results in superficial teaching and learning, [teachers] should limit their subject matter, striving to make it as meaningful as possible."[8] How else can teachers do this except under the specific direction of the Holy Spirit?

Christian teachers should constantly endeavor to improve their spiritual relationship to the Holy Spirit, their means of lesson preparation, their understanding of and concern for their pupils, and their ways of communicating spiritual truth. If teachers consider their God-given task of Christian teaching to involve eternal issues, they will constantly strive to improve.

Since the Spirit is always our Teacher, it is imperative that we always remain teachable.—Lewis Sperry Chafer[9]

To the extent that the Spirit is allowed to work freely in teachers, the teaching-learning process is facilitated, and Christian education goals are more readily attained.

THE HOLY SPIRIT AND METHODS

Does the use of teaching methods and materials nullify and rule out the work of the Holy Spirit? Can the Holy Spirit work through curricular materials, or should teachers simply teach "from the Bible"?

Methods are tools or ways of teaching; they are links for uniting content and experience. Methods are vehicles for bringing learners in vital contact with Christ and the Word. Method and message go hand in hand, as Bowman explains: "Some may express impatience with materials or methods as if they were an inconsequential, take-it-or-leave-it matter. But method and message go together. . . . Some may minimize techniques as ephemeral and unrelated to the timeless truths of religion. But the best we know about good methods traces back for its clues to the way the great Teacher taught as well as to what He said."[10]

Methods are not contrary to the working of the Spirit. Instead, they are "a description of how the Spirit works through the mind and how one may cooperate with the Spirit so that He may function freely."[11]

There are dangers, however, to avoid in the use of methods. Methods tend to become looked on as ends in themselves. And some teachers tend to use methods as substitutes for effort or preparation on their part. There is also the lurking danger that methods may substitute for the prime authority of God's scriptural revelation. Nelson Bell writes, "With the increased concern for the Sunday School, the scientific method of teaching . . . and with new concepts of communication, it becomes imperative that these and other advances or improvements be anchored to the divine revelation and not become a clever means of substituting human opinions for the clear affirmations of Scripture."[12]

Various methods may be used in teaching the Bible. These include storytelling, lectures, audio and visual aids, discussions, questions and answers, quizzes, reports, buzz groups, neighbor nudging, role playing, dramatizations, creative writing, interviews, brainstorming, panels, debates, projects, field trips, problem-solving, and many others.[13] In view of these and many other teaching approaches, the selection of methods is an important matter in Christian teaching.

In selecting a method consider these factors:

- time (in preparing and using the method),
- age of the students,
- purpose,
- ability or skill of the teacher,
- equipment and facilities, and
- lesson content.

The best method for any given occasion is the one that accomplishes the best results in the best way.

Pierce offers four questions a teacher may ask in evaluating a teaching method: "1. Did I *prepare* sufficiently in order to use this procedure to its best advantage? 2. Did I *use* this method in class in such a manner that it could work its best for the class? 3. Did the procedure actually *make its unique contribution* to class Bible study? 4. Did the procedure seem to *cause any change* in members toward the achieving of my larger teaching aim or sub-aim?"[14]

A major task of the Spirit in Christian teaching is guiding teachers in deciding the appropriate method or methods for the occasion at hand. The real Guide in Christian education is God the Spirit, and the methods of education are those He chooses to use. As you consciously depend on the Spirit in prayer and as you seek to be creative and effective in your teaching, He will guide you in choosing appropriate teaching techniques.

Therefore it is evident that methodology and the Holy Spirit are not incompatible. He works *through* methods to bring about spiritual nurture. The creative use of a variety of methods facilitates learning, and thus fosters spiritual change and maturation.

THE HOLY SPIRIT AND
PRINTED CURRICULAR MATERIALS

Whereas some teachers prefer to discard curricular materials and "just teach the Bible," most Christian educators recognize the inestimable value of printed materials as teaching aids. The effectiveness of the Spirit's ministry is increased as He works through prepared human instruments who are constantly sharpening their efficiency through the use of varied teaching tools, including printed materials. Good materials are certainly not incompatible with the Holy Spirit.

Through the proper use of curricular materials, teachers are better equipped to provide direction, continuity, and life-relatedness in their teaching. Printed materials can help teachers understand the content to be taught, as well as enhance their ability to communicate that content by means of creative methods suited specifically to the abilities and interests of the age-group being taught.

Of course, there are varying degrees of excellence and quality in printed materials. "What teachers should look for in printed manuals is the extent to which the writers help them apply scriptural principles to the local situation," LeBar suggests.[15] The Holy Spirit is related to printed materials in three ways: He guides writers and editors in the formulation of materials, He guides church leaders in the selection of materials, and He guides teachers in the use of materials—but only, of course, as those writers, editors, church leaders, and teachers rely on Him for His filling and guidance. Writers should seek the guidance of the Holy Spirit as they structure and write lessons that aim to meet the highest scriptural and educational standards. Their ministry is strategic because it involves the planning of content and procedures that can affect thousands of lives—teachers and students alike.

Church leaders should seek the guidance of the Spirit in selecting printed materials. Criteria for selecting material should include at least the following: "(1) Is the material in harmony with the objective sought? (2) Is it true to the Bible? (3) Does it contain [accurate] doctrinal views? (4) Is it prepared by scholarly and otherwise capable writers? (5) Is it suited to the needs and capacities of the pupils? (6) Can the teachers use it successfully? (7) Is it otherwise practical in the light of local conditions?"[16]

Of course, curricular materials must be adapted to local conditions. Teachers must adjust the materials to meet needs, and this too calls for the Spirit's guidance. Richards emphasizes this point. "A slavish reliance on printed plans, while helpful perhaps for an inexperienced teacher, cuts deeply into the potential for creativity. It's not hard to see why. Creative thinking is a process in which students are vitally involved. Often in this process, ideas are developed and needs revealed which no writer can plan for, nor teacher predict. The teacher has to feel free in such cases to respond to the lead of his class and spontaneously follow the guidance of the Holy Spirit. This may mean shortening some learning activities, adding unplanned ones, eliminating some that were planned."[17]

As teachers read their manuals, they should evaluate the suggestions in light of their own classes or groups. LeBar suggests that teachers ask the following questions as they adapt materials in lesson preparation: "Does the spirit of the whole meet the needs of my pupils? Should they be different people after studying these lessons? Do the aims seem to be pointed directly at them—deeply, personally? Would a slight change of focus do more for them? Is each lesson needed by them, or is there one aspect of the whole that is most urgently needed? Can I strengthen this emphasis without destroying the continuity of the series? Might it be wise to revamp a lesson or so in order to stress the needed emphasis?"[18]

These questions can best be answered as teachers rely on the Spirit of God in this preparatory step of teaching. Teachers will be better equipped to be led by the Spirit in adapting materials during the teaching process if they have already relied on Him in the study of materials written under the Spirit's guidance and selected under the Spirit's leadership. Thus will they be more capable instruments in making God's written revelation understood and experienced by their students.

With the dynamic power of God's Holy Spirit working within Christian teachers, on or within pupils, through creative methods and materials, to exalt Christ through His written Word, Christian education is a thrilling adventure.

What a crime for any session to be dull when it ought to be positively exciting, prosaic when it ought to be dynamic, boring when it ought to be a great adventure!—Lois E. LeBar[19]

The teaching-learning process can be spiritually dynamic and fruitful as Christian teachers cooperate with the blessed Holy Spirit in the glorious and rewarding ministry of Christian education!

WHAT WOULD YOU SAY?

1. If you spend time preparing your lessons, is this overriding the ministry of the Holy Spirit? Why or why not?

2. Why is it important that we know our students as individuals? Why is it important that we care for the students?

3. Which of the methods of teaching listed in this chapter have you used recently? Which ones not used could you plan to include in your teaching in the near future?

4. What are the strengths and weaknesses of the curricular materials you are using?

5. Are you relying on the Holy Spirit to guide you as you use and adapt teaching materials.

6. See pages 179–80 in my book *Teaching as Jesus Taught* for a list of fifty-seven teaching methods, and ask yourself, which of these can I use in my teaching? How will they enhance my students' learning?

PART FIVE
A BRIEF HISTORY OF
THE HOLY SPIRIT IN TEACHING

What place have leaders in church history attributed to the Holy Spirit in teaching? How do the religious circumstances of the times affect the doctrine of the Spirit's teaching ministry? To what extent have Christians in the past relied on the Holy Spirit for illumination, direction, and enablement?

This section is not intended as a survey of pneumatology (the doctrine of the Holy Spirit) nor as a history of Christian education.[1] It is simply a summary of one aspect of the doctrinal history of the Holy Spirit: His work as Teacher. Selected highlights from the early church period to modern times are discussed briefly.

CHAPTER 13
THE HOLY SPIRIT AND TEACHING
BEFORE THE REFORMATION

THE ANTE-NICENE PERIOD (PENTECOST TO A.D. 325)

Not many references to the Holy Spirit's ministry as a Teacher are to be
expected in the first few centuries of the church. Before the Council of
Nicaea (A.D. 325), written references to the Holy Spirit were made primarily in connection with doctrines. Concerning the subapostolic writers of
the first century and a half, Henry Swete writes: "There was as yet no
formal theology of the Spirit and no effort to create it; nor was there any
conscious heresy. But the presence of the Spirit in the body of Christ was
recognized on all hands as an acknowledged fact of the Christian life."[1]

In early controversial issues, attention was directed mainly to the
person of Christ. When controversy concerning the Holy Spirit did arise
(as the result of the presence of heresy), it dealt with His deity. The
Apostles' Creed, early hymns and liturgies, and direct statements of early
church fathers, such as Ignatius (died ca. 110), Clement of Rome (ca.
30–110), Justin Martyr (ca. 160–165), Irenaeus (ca. 130–200), Clement
of Alexandria (ca. 150–220), and Tertullian (ca. 160–220), affirmed the
deity and personality of the Spirit. The early church also referred (in
passing comments, more than in formal statements) to the authorship
of the Scriptures, regeneration, sanctification, and the future resurrection as works of the Holy Spirit.[2] He was also recognized as the source
of Christian knowledge.

The apocryphal *Shepherd of Hermas*, with its numerous references to the Spirit of God, is perhaps one of the earliest writings to speak of the Spirit's teaching ministry. "Hermas speaks also of the Holy Spirit as the Teacher and Sanctifier of believers in general."[3]

In his *Dialogue with Trypho,* Justin Martyr, an apologist writing in defense of Christianity, replied to Plato's belief that God can be known by the mind. Justin Martyr asked, "Will the human intellect ever see God unless it is furnished with the Holy Spirit?"[4] In the same work Justin Martyr stated that believers "receive, each one of them, gifts, according to their meetness, being illuminated through the name of this same Christ; for one receives the Spirit of understanding, and another the Spirit of counsel or strength or healing or foresight or teaching or of the fear of God."[5]

An interesting sidelight in gnostic heresy was the belief held by some of Marcion's followers that the other "Counselor" (John 14:16) was the apostle Paul!

One of the early references to the Spirit's teaching work came because of the rise of the Montanist heresy in the second and third centuries. Montanus and his followers held that they were the recipients of special revelation from the Spirit, who gave men truths in prophetic visions. Tertullian, a Montanist, was chiefly concerned, however, with the *teaching* work of the Spirit. He wrote: "The Paraclete, having many things to teach which the Lord reserved for Him . . . will first bear witness to Christ Himself . . . and glory Him and bring Him to our remembrance; and . . . He will proceed to reveal many things which appertain to the conduct of life."[6]

In his *Setting Forth of the Apostolic Preaching,* Irenaeus pointed out that it is through the Spirit that "the prophets prophesied, and the fathers learned the things of God, and the righteous were guided into the way of righteousness."[7]

Novatian's excellent tract on the Trinity referred to the Spirit as the Teacher of truth and Bestower of all spiritual gifts.[8]

Origen (185–254) stated that the Spirit enables men to acquire the gifts of learning, wisdom, and knowledge.[9]

That believers in the early church relied on the Holy Spirit's teaching is evident from these writers who commented on the Spirit's work as an important factor in the devotional life of the church.

THE NICENE AND POST-NICENE PERIODS (325–500)

The most significant doctrinal controversy of the early church revolved around Arius (ca. 250–336), who held that the Son and the Holy Spirit were created, and Athanasius (ca. 293–373), who affirmed their eternal existence and full deity. The controversy was climaxed at the Nicene Council in 325 when Arius was denounced and the phrase "I believe in the Holy Spirit" was stated in the Nicene Creed.

Following this heated conflict, the Arian leaders, interestingly, called attention to the teaching and sanctifying work of the Spirit. The second Sirmian Creed (357), for example, reads, "The Paraclete Spirit is through the Son, who was sent and came according to promise to instruct, teach, and sanctify the apostles and all believers."[10] Eunomius, an Arian, denied the deity and creative power of the Spirit but believed in His sanctifying and enlightening power.[11]

The Council at Constantinople (381) added to the Nicene Creed a statement on the procession of the Spirit from the Father. This was the result of an outburst of semi-Arian "Macedonians," who were attacked by the three Cappadocians, Basil of Caesarea (329–379), Gregory Nazianzen (330–389), and Gregory of Nyssa (ca. 335–395). Basil, in writing about the Holy Spirit, declared that He illuminates and gives people foreknowledge, the understanding of mysteries, and a share in spiritual gifts.

Frequent reference is made in the post-Nicene period to the Spirit's illuminating work. Athanasius referred to the Spirit as the illuminating living Energy and Gift of the Son.[12] Cyril of Jerusalem (died 386) frequently made mention of the Spirit as the Illuminator of the mind and soul in his *Catechetical Lectures* and *Mystogogic Lectures*. "He enlightens the soul and makes it see what is beyond human sight."[13] Theodoret (died 457) said that believers see the rays of light which stream from the Son only as those believers are enlightened by the Spirit. Without the Holy Spirit, according to Hilary of Poitiers (died 367), people would be unable to apprehend God and would even be destitute of the light of knowledge. Augustine (354–430) made this statement regarding knowledge and the work of the Spirit: "A man could not have wisdom, understanding, counsel, courage, knowledge, godliness, and the fear of God, unless he had received the Spirit of wisdom, understanding, counsel, courage, knowledge, godliness, and the fear of God."[14]

Gregory the Great (ca. 540–604), in writing of the Spirit's power to make a fisherman a preacher (Peter), a persecutor a teacher (Paul), and a publican an evangelist (Matthew), made these interesting statements: "Men are drawn to whatever the Spirit wills. They have no need to learn their new calling, as soon as he touches the mind, He teaches it. The mind is changed immediately as it falls under His enlightenment."[15]

The Council of Toledo (589) added the *filioque* phrase ("and the Son") to the creeds of Nicaea and Constantinople, indicating that the Western church believed in the procession of the Spirit from both the Father and the Son. The Greek Church did not accept this inclusion, and this difference was one of the major causes for the division of the East and West in 1054. "After the decline of this controversy the history of the doctrine is concerned chiefly with the work of the Holy Spirit rather than His Person."[16]

The Augustinian-Pelagian controversy has little bearing on the Spirit's task of teaching believers, because its chief debate was over Augustine's emphasis on the efficacious grace of the Holy Spirit versus Pelagius's view of the natural goodness of men without any need for the Spirit's redemptive work. However, Augustine, writing on education in his work *The Teacher*, said that people possess an innate capacity for truth.[17] He also wrote that the real Teacher of the Christian is the indwelling Christ.[18] Howard Grimes made this observation about Augustine's view of learning: "One does not learn religious truth through its being 'poured in,' as it were, from the outside; rather it is learned in the fullest sense only when it is a matter of inner apprehension."[19]

THE MIDDLE AGES (500–1500)

The hierarchical developments within the church in the Middle Ages led to a recognition, by many, of the Roman Catholic Church as the authority in spiritual matters. The Roman Church taught that it is the custodian and interpreter of the Scriptures. So conceived, the Scriptures were without the need of the Holy Spirit's illuminating work; and Christians were to be taught, if taught at all, by the church, not the Holy Spirit. "It was expressly denied that the Spirit could teach all Christians through the Word of God. Earthly priests were substituted for the Holy Spirit."[20]

The acceptance of doctrine on the basis of creedal statement, rather than on the basis of the written Word of God, led to rigid formalism and tradition. This tended to extinguish any flicker of vital interest in the Holy Spirit and His work. Intellectual and spiritual darkness prevailed, which led to moral poverty and corruption and thus to a virtual indifference to the things of the Spirit of God.

The powerlessness of the organized church led those interested in spiritual vitality to the excesses of mysticism. With its stress on direct, personal contact with God, mysticism naturally stressed the Holy Spirit's direct illumination on the mind and soul. Some of the medieval mystics were Bernard of Clairvaux (1090–1153), Hildegard (1098–1179), Hugo of St. Victor (1100–1141), Joachim (1132–1202), Johannes Eckhart (ca. 1260–1327), Occam (ca. 1285–1349), Heinrich Suso (1295–1366), John Tauler (1285–1361), John of Ruysbroeck (1291–1381), and St. Catherine of Siena (1342–1380). In the twelfth and thirteenth centuries, there existed groups of believers concerned with mysticism and the spiritual life known as the Cathari, also known as Albigenses.

Counteracting these mystical elements was Scholasticism, with its rationalistic approach, which obstructed interest in the Holy Spirit. Duns Scotus (ca. 1266–1308), Albertus Magnus (ca. 1200–1280), and Thomas Aquinas (ca. 1225–1274) were representative figures. Of interest is the fact that, according to Rees, "Aquinas treats the whole subject of revelation without referring to the Spirit."[21] Aquinas wrote this about God as Teacher: "Just as a doctor, although he works exteriorly while nature alone works interiorly, is said to cause healing, so man is said to teach, although he announces exteriorly while God teaches interiorly."[22] Teaching, like medicine, is an art, according to Aquinas. A doctor and a teacher "ply their art, by imitating and perfecting nature."[23] And in that process the teacher must "be guided by the nature of the learner, who, learning by discovery, proceeds to a knowledge of the unknown by relating it to his present knowledge."[24]

The failure of the Crusades in the twelfth and thirteenth centuries dulled spiritual zeal, and philosophical interests squelched a concern for the inner teaching ministry of the Holy Spirit.

WHAT'S YOUR OPINION?

1. In the first few centuries of the church, not many writers referred to the Holy Spirit as a Teacher. Do you think this is true today? If so, why is this? What accounts for an absence of attention to this aspect of the Holy Spirit's work?
2. Would you agree with Augustine's statement that religious truth is learned not "from the outside [but] in the fullest sense only when it is a matter of inner apprehension"?
3. What factors in the Middle Ages led to a neglect of the Holy Spirit's teaching ministry? How did the mysticism of the Middle Ages relate to that neglect? Was mysticism a proper response?
4. What do you think of Aquinas's idea that teachers are like doctors?

CHAPTER 14
THE HOLY SPIRIT AND TEACHING
FROM THE REFORMATION TO THE PRESENT

THE PROTESTANT REFORMATION

More than a century ago, George Smeaton observed, "The period of the Reformation . . . gives a testimony to the Holy Spirit more full and explicit than had ever been uttered since the Apostolic Age."[1] The sovereignty of God, the depravity of man, the authority of the Bible, efficacious grace, and justification by faith were doctrines emphasized in the Reformation.

Reformers were concerned with the work of the Holy Spirit in four specific areas: regeneration, illumination, the Scriptures, and church ordinances. The Reformers taught that regeneration comes by the efficacious grace of God's Spirit, not through the church. In place of the priestly sacerdotalism of the Roman Catholic Church, the doctrine of the priesthood of all believers—the right to read and interpret the Scriptures individually and privately—was taught by the Reformers.

According to the Reformers, the Holy Spirit in illumination opens the minds and hearts of believers to receive the Word of God. Sometimes the ministry of illumination seemed to be considered a part of regeneration. John Calvin (1509–1564) wrote, "By His Spirit illuminating their minds and forming their hearts to the love and cultivation of righteousness, He makes them new creatures."[2] Calvin also related illumination to (or identified it with) the Spirit's "inner testimony," His work whereby He convinces the sinner at salvation of the certainty of the truth of Scripture.[3]

The first Helvetic Confession (1536), a Reformation creed, makes a similar point: "In regeneration the understanding is enlightened by the Holy Spirit to understand both the mysteries and the will of God, and the will itself is not only charged by the Spirit, but also furnished with powers both to will and to do good spontaneously (Rom. 8:5–6)."[4]

Martin Luther (1483–1546) and Calvin both said much about the Holy Spirit's relationship to the Bible. Luther strongly opposed the "enthusiasts" or "spiritualists" of his day (of whom Carlstadt, whose real name was Andrews Bodenstein, was a leading proponent), who taught that the Spirit works apart from or beyond the Scriptures. Regin Prenter has written an entire book describing Luther's controversy with the enthusiasts.[5] Luther, however, taught that the Spirit and the Word are so intimately joined that the Spirit never goes beyond the written Word.

Calvin taught that the Word of God has "no efficacy unless at the same time the Holy Spirit works in the hearts of the hearers, creating faith and making men's minds open to receive the Word."[6] Calvin did not teach that the Spirit causes Scripture to become the Word of God, as Wilhelm Niesel, a neoorthodox interpreter of Calvin, seems to say.[7] Instead, Calvin taught that the Holy Spirit testifies to the heart of believers that the objective body of truth is of divine origin and authoritatively true. This is the Spirit's "inner testimony." Apart from this work of the Spirit at salvation, a person cannot properly interpret the Scriptures (1 Cor. 2:14).

The Holy Spirit, Calvin affirmed, works alongside the written Word and not apart from it. "It is no less reasonable to boast of the Spirit without the Word, than it would be an absurd thing to bring forward the Word without the Spirit."[8]

Whereas Luther taught that the Spirit cannot make Christ real without the preceding ministry of the preached word, Calvin held that the Spirit can illuminate "in an internal manner . . . without the intervention of any preaching."[9] Both men, of course, agreed that the Spirit works through the written Word, never apart from it and never beyond it. Calvin wrote that "the Word is the instrument by which the Lord disperses the illumination of His Spirit to believers."[10] Calvin also emphasized that the Spirit, besides enlightening and convincing a person at the moment of regeneration, also illumines the believer in the process of sanctification.

Though not referring often in his writings to the teaching work of the Holy Spirit, Ulrich Zwingli (1484–1531), reformer in Zurich, Switzerland, was concerned about education. He said that the goal of education is "to render the student as much like Christ as possible."[11] Like Luther and Calvin, he taught that the Holy Spirit works in conjunction with the Word, not apart from it.

THE ANABAPTISTS AND THE REFORMATION

The Anabaptists were a force in the Reformation whose input is often unrecognized. They were severely harassed and persecuted by the main Reformers and their followers as well as by state officials because a number of their views differed from those of the Reformers and state leaders. They are little known because, being persecuted, they had little time for writing.

The movement began in Switzerland with Conrad Grebel, Felix Manz, and George Blaurock on January 21, 1525, when these men broke from Zwingli, under whom they had studied. They rejected infant baptism, which all the major Reformers had been unwilling to do. The Swiss Brethren, as they called themselves, were dubbed by their enemies as Anabaptists ("Rebaptizers"), because they had been baptized as infants but were rebaptized as adult believers. This break from the major Reformers also involved a break from the state church. According to the Reformers, people became members of the state church by infant baptism. But according to the Anabaptists only adults who had experienced personal salvation in Christ and then had been baptized could become members of the Anabaptist gatherings. Thus these local churches, consisting of baptized adult believers, were totally separate from the one state church. Such a concept in that day was radical. Yet the Anabaptists were vigorous in their concern for a purified New Testament church, loyalty to the Bible, and a life of humility, purity, and obedience to Christ.

Many people misunderstood the Anabaptists by confusing them with the spiritualists or inspirationists. Thomas Muntzer and his Zwickau prophets, for example, were thought of by Luther and others as typical of the Anabaptists. This, however, was a false association. The inspirationists believed that immediate illumination by the Holy Spirit was more important than the Bible. They claimed that God gave them special revelation beyond the Scriptures. Nor did they have much concern for the visible church. In this they differed from the Anabaptists.

Because of this socially revolutionary concept of a church separate from state legislation and their rejection of infant baptism, the Anabaptists for more than 150 years were captured, tortured, imprisoned, and executed in Switzerland, Germany, Austria, Moravia, and the Netherlands. Hundreds of them were burned at the stake, drowned, or beheaded, all because they were considered seditionists. Others were deported from their homelands.[12]

Though persecution kept many Anabaptists from writing lengthy theologies, they did state their beliefs in early confessions, sermons, hymns, and letters.[13] Like the major Reformers, they emphasized the work of the Holy Spirit in the believer's life and in relationship to the Scriptures. For example, Balthasar Hubmaier, the first Anabaptist theologian, wrote in 1526, "I believe also in the Holy Spirit . . . in whom I set all my trust that He will teach me all truth, increase my faith, and kindle the fire of love in my heart."[14]

Pilgram Marpeck (died 1556), an influential Anabaptist theologian in South Germany, emphasized in his *Twelve Articles* (1526–1527) that the Holy Spirit "strengthens God's people. He is the Comforter. He is 'the One who guides into all truth.' . . . He personally dwells in the believer."[15]

The Schleitheim Confession, composed by Michael Sattler in 1527, begins with a reference to the Trinity and "the gifts of the Spirit who is sent from the Father to all believers for their strength and comfort and for their perseverance in all tribulation."[16]

Several Anabaptist leaders wrote that every believer has the Holy Spirit and is therefore capable of understanding the Scriptures.

Hans Denck, a scholarly and controversial leader in South Germany, wrote in 1526 that without the Spirit one looks for light in the Scriptures but finds only darkness.[17]

Jacob Hutter, leader of the Moravian Anabaptists, who was burned at the stake in 1536, wrote in the year before his death that Christians are "ruled, instructed, taught, and led in all truth" by the Word through "the light and brilliance of [God's] Holy Spirit."[18]

Peter Reidemann (1506–1556), a Moravian Hutterite missionary, wrote two confessions of his beliefs, one in each of two imprisonments. In his second *Rechenschaft*, in 1541, he wrote, "Just as breath determines the word and gives it shape and sound, so does the breath, wind, and Spirit of God make the Word living and active within us."[19]

Menno Simons (1472–1559), the leader of the Dutch Anabaptists, after whom the Mennonites are named, emphasized the Trinity. He too stated (in 1550) that the Spirit "guides us into all truth."[20] Another Dutch leader, Dirk Philips, said that "believers are enlightened by the Spirit of truth."[21]

It is obvious from this brief survey of the Reformers' and Anabaptists' views on the teaching work of the Holy Spirit that "the developed doctrine of the work of the Holy Spirit is an exclusively Reformation doctrine."[22]

THE POST-REFORMATION PERIOD

The Reformation had freed many people from the bondage of Roman Catholicism. However, the Reformation, along with the intellectual and cultural interests of the Renaissance (which had been catalyzed by the expanding influence of the Crusades, the universities, and commerce), gave rise to the excesses of independent thinking in the seventeenth and eighteenth centuries. People's accomplishments led them to place undue confidence in themselves and their abilities. This found its peak of expression in subjectivism—the attitude that places authority in human religious feeling (mystical or emotional subjectivism) or in human reason (rationalistic subjectivism). The former type of subjectivism sometimes appealed to the Holy Spirit apart from the Scriptures; the latter rejected both the Spirit and the Scriptures.

The Puritan movement in England stressed the need for holy living through the direct teaching work of the Spirit, which was associated with the intuitive perceptions of the soul. The place of intuitive immediacy led to an attitude of disdain toward reasoning, study, and education. The Puritans believed that they could be taught by the Holy Spirit directly, apart from intermediary helps such as human teachers, methods, books, or even the Bible.[23]

Rationalism took the form of deism in England, skepticism in Germany, and atheism in France. Within this intellectual soil the roots of philosophic rationalism were planted; they blossomed later in the nineteenth century in the form of liberal theology. Obviously the work of the Holy Spirit as Teacher was entirely neglected in this intellectual climate.

Reaction to Puritanism led to ecclesiasticism in the Church of England, which, in turn, was met with the protest of Quakerism against cold sacramentalism and formal religion. With their emphasis on the Holy Spirit as the "inner light" of the soul, the Quakers said there was no need for the Scriptures. Robert Barclay, a disciple of Quaker founder George Fox, wrote that "the testimony of the Spirit is that alone by which the true knowledge of God hath been, is, and can be only revealed."[24] Along with the Quakers' claim to the "immediate consciousness" of the Spirit's revealing work came extravagant claims to "immediate leadings" by the Spirit in everyday activities.

Pietism in Germany shared some similar convictions. Jacob Boehme (1575–1624), a leading Pietist, professed a unique spiritual insight into divine mysteries. According to him, those who possess this illumination and are therefore children of light have within them the Holy Spirit moving and reigning and teaching them all things.[25] But not all Pietists held that view. Philip Spener (1635–1705) and his student August Hermann Francke (1663–1727) placed more emphasis on devotion and practical Christian living than on doctrine, a reaction against scholastic Lutheranism and theology as mere erudition.[26] Yet Francke "made the Scriptures . . . the subject of most of his lectures . . . applying them to the hearts and consciences of his pupils."[27]

The revival movement under John Wesley (1703–1791) and George Whitefield (1714–1770) in England and America restored a needed emphasis on regeneration by the Spirit. Wesley taught the necessity of the Spirit for holy living and for guidance into all truth.

The Swiss educator Johann H. Pestalozzi (1747–1827) said that humankind, like nature, is inherently good. Children are born with a propensity for goodness and benevolence, not with original sin. Moral corruption, then, stems from the influence of one's social environment. He emphasized the importance of feelings and relationships in the educational process and deemphasized "cold" memorization of catechisms and creeds.

A favorable emotional climate between teacher and students, and among students, is essential if one is to advance intellectually. While his emphasis on a loving and creative atmosphere in the classroom is commendable, his humanitarian pietism and stress on inherent moral goodness left no place for the ministry of the Holy Spirit or the Scriptures in education.

MODERN TIMES

In the nineteenth and twentieth centuries the doctrine of the teaching ministry of the Spirit has been treated variously. Friedrich Schleiermacher's "religion of feeling" (1768–1834) denied the personality of the Spirit. This restoration of the heresy of Sabellianism had no place for the Spirit as Teacher. And the theology of Albrecht Ritschl (1822–1889) lacked any significant and pure presentation of the doctrine of the Holy Spirit.

In the nineteenth century the theological world was greatly influenced by German rationalistic philosophy, the evolutionary theory, higher criticism of the Bible, and optimistic postmillennialism. Tenets of liberal theology, including the denial of the personality of the Spirit, were widely held. Revivalism under the leadership of Jonathan Edwards (1703–1758), Charles Finney (1792–1875), D. L. Moody (1837–1899), and others stressed the power of the Spirit in salvation; but this did comparatively little to help believers formulate a clear concept of the Holy Spirit as the Teacher of divine truth in Christian hearts. Evangelism was stressed far more than education or edification, though the presence of converts provided a situation ripe for a work of education.

Horace Bushnell (1802–1876) reacted to revivalism and especially its appeals to children. In Christian homes, children, he said, are in the covenant of promise[28] and therefore are to be nurtured, not converted.[29] But children from non-Christian homes, he said, need to be regenerated, and that work is by the Holy Spirit. Bushnell stressed the significant role parents have in educating their children. His optimistic view of human nature and his concern for education by experience rather than by transmitting content influenced religious education in the decades ahead.

The twentieth century is marked with interesting developments in the study of the relationship of the Holy Spirit to Christian education.

Basically, four theological positions have dominated the American "Christian" scene in this century, each of which has had direct bearing on religious education. They are liberalism, neoorthodoxy, neoliberalism, and evangelicalism.

LIBERALISM

The teaching of old liberalism, which had its heyday in the first three decades of the century, included an optimistic belief in the goodness of humanity, a utopian outlook toward human society, an emphasis on the indwelling presence of God with little stress on His sovereignty, a rejection of the finality of biblical revelation, and an acceptance of a unitarian concept of Jesus Christ as a man but not God. All this, as can easily be seen, left no place for the work of the Holy Spirit in regeneration or Christian experience. A rejection of the deity of Jesus Christ meant a virtual dismissal of a belief in the Trinity, with an accompanying disregard for the Holy Spirit as the divine Teacher, possessing full deity and personality, operative in the hearts of individuals to redeem and instruct.

Liberal religious educators shared the same doctrinal viewpoints. Progressive religious education began to thrive in that very theological atmosphere, along with the endorsement of Dewey's empirical approach to education.

A belief in human goodness led educators to have more interest in student growth patterns and human development than in lesson content. An optimistic view toward society meant that religious education became socially organized and that social values were regarded more highly than spiritual values. The belief in divine immanence resulted in a blurring of distinctions between the operations of the human and divine elements in Christian education.

George Albert Coe (1862–1951), the foremost spokesman of liberal religious education in the early twentieth century and an able theorist of progressive religious education, did much to introduce Dewey's experience-centered approach to religious education. Coe may well be called "the John Dewey of religious education," though naturalism was not his basic religious principle. While Dewey taught that learning is the continous reconstruction of experience, Coe was saying that "continuous reconstruction is . . . the essence of the divine work in and through the human."[30]

Such an outlook toward religious education involved a repudiation of the Holy Spirit's teaching ministry on three crucial counts.

First, the denial of original sin and the avowal of humankind's natural goodness meant that character could be produced by proper environmental influences, which, in turn, did away with any need for supernatural instruction. One can see similarities here to Johann Pestalozzi's views. Frank Gaebelein aptly described this weakness: "The fatal error of Protestant liberalism in dealing with character education lies in its substitution of [a] psychological method for the work of the Holy Spirit. Only the Spirit of God can make Christians. And He does it through His sovereign use of the truth set forth in Scripture."[31]

Second, the methodology of progressive religious education repudiated the need for the supernatural teaching of the Spirit. Experience-centered education emphasized progressive growth and questioned the necessity of the Holy Spirit's redemptive work.

Third, an inadequate view of values left the teacher with no absolute realities to teach. The only concern of the religious liberal educator was to reconstruct religion by releasing the students' creative religious experiences. Adhering to Dewey's principle of relative values influenced religious educators to reject the Christian view of the finality of biblical revelation.

NEOORTHODOXY

The second major theological position is neoorthodoxy. James Smart, a neoorthodox religious educator, describes the situation that gave birth to its exposure in America:

> Liberal optimism about human nature was shattered by the outbreak of startling forms of inhumanity within Western civilization. Modern man, confronted by evil in its naked reality, began to find the biblical description of it once more believable. The idea of an inevitable progress of the human race no longer carried conviction, and the corollary belief, that divinity is to be identified with

the natural process by which man moves toward the fulfillment of his destiny, seemed hard to distinguish from a humanism in which all belief in God is abandoned. The bankruptcy of unreconstructed liberalism was impossible to conceal, and the exposure was helped forward by theologians such as [Karl] Barth (1886–1968), and [Emil] Brunner (1889–1966) in Europe, and Reinhold Niebuhr (1892–1971) in America.[32]

When the utopian hopes of liberalism were shattered by two world wars, neoorthodoxy found a solid footing in American theological soil. But what did it teach concerning the Holy Spirit? And how has religious education reacted to it as a theological movement?

Neoorthodoxy restored an emphasis on the utter desperation of mankind's depraved nature, the absolute "otherness" of God's sovereign transcendence, and the centrality of revelation. However, it is still far from orthodox evangelicalism. The Bible, says the neoorthodox theologian, is not to be equated with the Word of God. The Bible merely *contains* the Word of God and is a record of past revelation. It is a human book, containing errors, and it becomes the Word of God only when it speaks personally to its readers. According to neoorthodoxy God's revelation is His supernatural breaking into history through an individual's personal encounter with Jesus Christ. The Holy Spirit is the existential, subjective operation of God, making His revelation become truth to individuals.[33] The Spirit prepares people to receive the revelation of God.

Emil Brunner was in direct conflict with liberal religious education when he stated that the life of faith does not belong to the sphere of education but is higher than education. Harrison Elliott writes that, according to Brunner, "the Christian faith cannot be interpreted through educational processes."[34] Education does have a place, according to Brunner, but a minor one. It is the "human carrier for the proclamation of the 'Word of God.' . . . But the understanding and acceptance of the divine revelation to the Christian experience which is thus made possible are not dependent upon such an educational process. Indeed, what is happening in the experience of the individuals who have the 'Word' proclaimed to them through an educational process is in an entirely different and separate realm."[35]

Liberal religious educators reacted strongly against the inroads of this "new theology." Coe was one of the first to write against it.[36] Yet an increasing number of religious educators accepted neoorthodoxy as their theological frame of reference. In fact, Sara Little refers to neoorthodox Christian education as "the new philosophy of Christian education."[37] This position was represented by educators such as Iris V. Cully, James D. Smart, and D. Campbell Wyckoff. They placed an emphasis on the Bible in teaching but still maintained the erroneous neoorthodox view toward the Bible. (See chapter 8 for a critique of neoorthodox Christian education.)

NEOLIBERALISM

The third major theological platform in the twentieth century is neoliberalism. Neoorthodoxy so undermined the foundational tenets of "old" liberalism that many liberals have reconstructed their theology into what is called neoliberalism. The classic work representing such a move among liberal educators was H. Shelton Smith's *Faith and Nurture*, written in 1941, in which his purpose was to "reconstruct ... theological foundations in light of more realistic insights of current Christian faith."[38] Neoliberals stress the greatness and grace of God, the dual nature of people as children of God and fallen creatures, the centrality of revelation, and the reconciling work of Christ.[39] Many refer to the Holy Spirit as the "agent" operative in the church. In 1980 Randolph Crump Miller wrote *The Theory of Christian Education Practice*,[40] in which he advocates process theology (a liberal view that God is finite and that He is both actual and potential), naturalism, and existentialism (that truth is found in a person's own experiences).[41]

In recent days a movement known as postmodernism has become prominent in some circles. In this view objective truth is nonexistent; the Bible's narratives are fictional, not factual; intuition and feelings can tell more about reality than reason can; moral standards vary from culture to culture and are therefore relative. Obviously such an approach to the truth, the Bible, reason, and morals has little place for an infallible Bible and the supernatural ministry of the Holy Spirit.[42]

EVANGELICALISM

The fourth theological platform of twentieth century America is evangelicalism. In the first several decades of this century, evangelicals were staunch in their defense of orthodox truths against the insipid doctrines of liberalism. Doctrinal rectitude was stressed, and Bible teachers were concerned primarily with transmitting scriptural truth.

Liberals reacted against this emphasis on content, because to them it spelled sterile orthodoxy and routine, lifeless transmission of content. But liberals, on the other hand, placed the student and his experiences, instead of the Word of God, at the center of the educational orbit. Thus this liberal emphasis, just as much as so-called transmissivism, failed to see the need for the dynamic spiritual power of the Holy Spirit, energizing every phase of the teaching-learning process.

Today, most evangelical Christian educators are seeing the need for giving due regard to both biblical content *and* the Holy Spirit's ministry in the educational process. To evangelicals, the Bible is the basic content to be transmitted in Christian education, but God's Spirit provides the spiritual power so essential for communicating His truth effectively.

TO REFLECT ON

1. The Reformers said that the Holy Spirit and the written Word of God work together. What do you think of this? Is it possible for the Holy Spirit to teach believers spiritual truths apart from the Scriptures? Why or why not?
2. What were the strengths and weaknesses of the Puritans' views on the Holy Spirit?
3. How did liberalism's optimistic view of human nature influence religious education?
4. What are the weaknesses in neoorthodoxy and neoliberalism?

CHAPTER 15
CHALLENGE:
TEACH!

W HEN A TEACHER RECOGNIZES that the work of God the Holy Spirit is indispensable in the teaching-learning process, teaching takes on exciting dimensions.

Following are five implications stemming from, or summarizing, this study.

REMEMBER THAT CHRISTIAN EDUCATION
IS A SUPERNATURAL TASK

The presence of God's Holy Spirit in teaching takes Christian education beyond mere programming, methodology, and techniques. The Spirit's work in education makes it a divine, supernatural ministry.

Christian education takes on new perspective when viewed as God's work, not man's, as the energy of the Spirit, not of the flesh. Seen as a divine work, teaching God's truths becomes a responsibility of fantastic proportions and implications. As you acknowledge the work of the Spirit, you sense that Christian education involves high objectives, a holy Book, divine truths, eternal souls, heavenly issues, and an infallible Teacher. As LeBar has aptly stated, "How superlative ought to be any form of Christian teaching, with so many supernatural distinctives—the infallible written Word revealing our Creator-Redeemer God who sent His Son to be King of kings, and the Holy Spirit working within the teacher, upon or within the pupils, to exalt the Saviour through the inscripturated record!"[1]

Teaching the Word in the wisdom and power of the Spirit becomes a great adventure with the master Teacher Himself.—Lois E. LeBar[2]

Chafer eloquently discusses two reasons why the Spirit's teaching is supernaturally sublime:

> There is no didactic discipline in the world comparable to the teaching of Christ by the Holy Spirit, both because of the fact that infinity characterizes the themes which are taught, and because of the Teacher's method of approach by which He, by the Spirit, enters the innermost recesses of the heart where impressions originate and there not only tells out the truth of transcendent magnitude, but causes the pupil actually to grasp the things thus revealed. "By faith we understand" (Heb. 11:3). That Christ would continue the teaching begun while here on earth was clearly promised (John 16:12–15), and implied in Acts 1:1 where reference is made to "all that Jesus began both to do and to teach."[3]

RELY ON THE HOLY SPIRIT

Teachers are effective only to the extent that they rely on and are yielded to the Holy Spirit. Though Christian education is a divine task, it is also a process involving humans, a process in which teachers must cooperate with God, rather than work against Him. Seen in the light of the Spirit's teaching ministry, Christian education suggests that teachers be submissive to the Spirit in lesson preparation and be ready for His guidance during class sessions. LeBar forcefully depicts the matter of yieldedness to the Spirit.

> Only a tool, only a channel are we in the hands of God. Yes, in one sense; yet both these figures are inadequate because tools and channels are dead and mechanical while human instruments have

wills of their own. The Lord does not purpose to deaden our wills or render them mechanical, but to activate them under His control. He does not propose to break our wills, for we shall need the full force of them in our struggle against evil. He wants us deliberately to identify our wills with His.

This will mean the total submission of the old self-life with its longings and strivings. This means that we shall be constantly looking to Him rather than around us, constantly listening to Him when it is more natural to talk, constantly obeying His slightest indication without question.[4]

The need for dependence on the Spirit of God is one factor that makes Christian education distinct from secular education. According to Bell, "It is the need for supernatural help that places both teacher and pupil in a position unknown in the secular field."[5]

RELATE GOD'S WORD TO STUDENTS' EXPERIENCES

The Holy Spirit has given God's Holy Word— the content of Christian education—but, in addition, He is concerned that the truths of God's written revelation become personally appropriated by the students. A proper understanding of the educational work of the Holy Spirit provides Christian teachers with a balanced, blended approach to the question of content and experience. Only by the Holy Spirit is subject matter effectively transmitted to the students, the written Word made a part of one's experience, and propositional truths made personal.[6]

REST SATISFIED WITH
NOTHING LESS THAN SPIRITUAL RESULTS

The goals of teaching, as suggested by the biblical doctrine on the Spirit's teaching, are more than acquisition of knowledge, the establishment of educational programs, or the use of effective techniques. As a divine task of God's Spirit, Christian education is the communication of God's truth to secure students' wholehearted conformity to God's will.

Effective teachers evaluate what results they are or are not gaining and strive to see spiritual results—that is, results of the Spirit—accomplished. They ask themselves, "What kind of results am I getting?" Teachers cannot assume that they are automatically getting spiritual results. They must constantly test their teaching, while at the same time depending on the Spirit for spiritual fruit.

RECOGNIZE THAT IN THE FINAL SENSE GOD THE HOLY SPIRIT IS THE TEACHER

It is God who does the teaching. The Bible teacher is a channel of His grace, an instrument doing the planting and watering. The growth is from God (1 Cor. 3:6). The spiritual effectiveness of Christian teaching rests ultimately with God the Spirit. Every Christian teacher and pupil ought to pray in the words of David, "Teach me your way, O LORD" (Ps. 27:11). Before God can teach students through a teacher, that teacher must first be taught by Him. Then with the psalmist the instructor can say, "You yourself have taught me" (119:102). (Other verses that speak of God as Teacher are Pss. 71:17; 86:11; 94:12; Isa. 28:26; 48:17.) Elihu triumphantly exalted God as Teacher by the rhetorical question, "Who is a teacher like Him?" (Job 36:22).

The dynamic work of the Holy Spirit in teaching is what makes Christian education a glorious work. This is what makes the teaching of God's holy truths a noble, and at the same time enjoyable, task.

The compelling words of our resurrected Lord call for His followers to "make disciples." And this task, He said, involves "baptizing them . . . and teaching them" (Matt. 28:19–20). His commissioning words call for dedication to an *educational* ministry.

Teach *confidently,* empowered by the Holy Spirit, your Teacher.

Teach *joyously,* realizing you are in partnership with the blessed Holy Spirit in a divine-human process.

Teach *purposefully,* with the goal of spiritual transformation, growth, and change before you.

Teach *creatively,* aware of the principles of teaching and learning, the means by which God the Spirit helps others learn.

Teach *reverently,* grateful that you are privileged to study and communicate God's inspired, authoritative Word.

Teach *convincingly,* assured that you are engaged in the greatest task in the world: introducing others to the written Word and the living Word, God's Book and God's Son!

TO PUT INTO ACTION

1. In what sense is Christian education a supernatural work?
2. Do you sense the significance of your teaching ministry as a matter of cooperating with God the Holy Spirit? In what ways do you need to cultivate that concept of your being a partner with the Holy Spirit?

ENDNOTES

CHAPTER 1—POWER IN YOUR TEACHING

1. Lois E. LeBar, *Education That Is Christian*, rev. ed. (Wheaton, Ill.: Victor, 1995), 15.
2. Carl F. H. Henry, "Divine Revelation and the Bible," in *Inspiration and Interpretation*, ed. John F. Walvoord (Grand Rapids: Eerdmans, 1957), 256.
3. Ibid., 257.
4. Brian Richardson, "Do Bible Facts Change Attitudes?" *Bibliotheca Sacra* 140 (April–June 1983): 163–72.
5. Ibid., 168.
6. Findley B. Edge, *Teaching for Results*, rev. ed. (Nashville: Broadman & Holman, 1995).
7. Andrew Murray, *The Spirit of Christ: Thoughts on the Indwelling of the Holy Spirit in the Believer and the Church* (London: Nisbet, n.d.), 219.
8. James DeForest Murch, *Christian Education and the Local Church*, rev. ed. (Cincinnati: Standard, 1958), 155–56.
9. James Michael Lee, "Toward a New Era: A Blueprint for Positive Action," in *The Religious Education We Need*, ed. James Michael Lee (Mishawaka, Ind.: Religious Education, 1977), 130–31.
10. Richardson, "Do Bible Facts Change Attitudes?" 168.

11. J. Theodore Mueller, "The Holy Spirit and the Scriptures," in *Revelation and the Bible,* ed. Carl F. H. Henry (Grand Rapids: Baker, 1958), 276.

12. Wilhelm Wiswedel, "Bible: Inner and Outer Word," in *Mennonite Encyclopedia,* ed. Harold S. Bender (Hillsboro, Kan.: Mennonite Brethren), 1 (1955): 326.

13. Charles Hodge, *Systematic Theology* (Grand Rapids: Eerdmans, 1960), 3:472–73.

14. Ronald S. Wallace, *Calvin's Doctrine of the Word and Sacrament* (Grand Rapids: Eerdmans, 1957), 128–29.

15. John Calvin, *Commentary on a Harmony of the Evangelists, Matthew, Mark, and Luke,* trans. William Pringle (reprint, Grand Rapids: Baker, 1981), 3:375.

16. W. H. Griffith Thomas, *Ministerial Life and Work* (Grand Rapids: Baker, 1974), 82.

CHAPTER 2—THE TITLES OF THE HOLY SPIRIT
AS A TEACHER

1. John F. Walvoord, *The Holy Spirit,* rev. ed. (Grand Rapids: Zondervan, 1958), 10–11. Also see James Elder Cummings, *Through the Eternal Spirit* (London: Marshall, Morgan & Scott, 1937), 36–37.

2. Franz Delitzsch, "Isaiah," in *Commentary on the Old Testament in Ten Volumes,* by C. F. Keil and F. Delitzsch (Grand Rapids: Eerdmans, 1982), 7:282.

3. Brooke Foss Westcott, *The Gospel according to St. John: The Authorized Version with Introduction and Notes* (London: Murray, 1890), 230; Fenton J. A. Hort, quoted in Henry Barclay Swete, *The Holy Spirit in the New Testament* (reprint, Grand Rapids: Baker, 1976), 155; and J. D. Ryle, *Ryle's Expository Thoughts on John* (Grand Rapids: Zondervan, n.d.), 2:304.

4. John Peter Lange, "John," in *Lange's Commentary on the Holy Scriptures* (reprint, Grand Rapids: Zondervan, n.d.), 18:442. Also see W. Hall Harris, "A Theology of John's Writings," in *A Biblical Theology of the New Testament,* ed. Roy B. Zuck (Chicago: Moody, 1994), 200.

5. Westcott, *The Gospel according to St. John,* 212.

6. E. Y. Mullins, "Paraclete," in *International Standard Bible Encyclopedia*, 4 (1949), 2245. See also J. R. Michaels, "Paraclete," in *International Standard Bible Encyclopedia*, 3 (1986), 659–60.

7. Westcott, *The Gospel according to St. John*, 213; Hermann Cremer, *Biblico-Theological Lexicon of the New Testament Greek*, trans. William Urwick, 4th ed. (Edinburgh: Clark, 1895), 338; and R. C. H. Lenski, *The Interpretation of St. John's Gospel* (Minneapolis: Augsburg, 1961), 998.

8. Julius Charles Hare, *The Mission of the Comforter*, 2d ed. (Boston: Gould S. Lincoln, 1854), 309.

9. This is also the preference of William Hendriksen (*Exposition of the Gospel according to John*, New Testament Commentary [Grand Rapids: Baker, 1953], 276) and of Barnabas Lindars (*The Gospel of John* [London: Oliphants, 1972], 479).

10. Clement Clemance, *The Scripture Doctrine of the Holy* Spirit (London: John Snow, 1887), 42. George Johnston argues against the rather unusual view of Sigmund Mowinckel and Otto Betz that the Paraclete is an angel (*The Spirit-Paraclete in the Gospel of John* [Cambridge: University Press, 1970], 96–118).

11. Raymond E. Brown has an extended discussion on the Paraclete (*The Gospel according to John* [Garden City, N.Y.: Doubleday, 1970], 2:1135–44). Also see Leon Morris, *The Gospel according to John* (Grand Rapids: Eerdmans, 1971), 662–66; and Westcott, *The Gospel according to St. John*, 211–13.

12. E. K. Simpson and F. F. Bruce, *Commentary on the Epistles to the Ephesians and the Colossians*, New International Commentary on the New Testament (Grand Rapids: Eerdmans, 1957), 37–38.

13. S. D. F. Salmond, "The Epistle to the Ephesians," in *The Expositor's Greek Testament* (Grand Rapids: Eerdmans, 1951), 3:273–74; and Francis Faulker, *The Epistle of Paul to the Ephesians: An Introduction and Commentary* (Grand Rapids: Eerdmans, n.d.), 60.

14. Albert Barnes, *Barnes' Notes on the New Testament* (Grand Rapids: Kregel, 1962), 975.

15. C. Fred Dickason, "The Holy Spirit in Teaching," in *Introduction to Biblical Christian Education*, ed. Werner C. Graendorf (Chicago: Moody, 1981), 115.

16. Ibid.

CHAPTER 3—THE TEACHING MINISTRIES
OF THE HOLY SPIRIT

1. Lewis Sperry Chafer, *He That Is Spiritual* (1918; rev. ed., Grand Rapids: Zondervan, 1967), 62.

2. G. G. Findlay, "St. Paul's First Epistle to the Corinthians," in *The Expositor's Greek Testament,* 2:784.

3. Lange, "John," 18:445.

4. Swete, *The Holy Spirit in the New Testament,* 153.

5. Archibald Thomas Robertson, *Word Pictures in the New Testament* (Nashville: Broadman, 1930), 4:89.

6. Homer S. Kent, Jr., *Light in the Darkness* (Grand Rapids: Baker, 1974), 176, 187.

7. Merrill C. Tenney, "The Gospel of John," in *The Expositor's Bible Commentary* (Grand Rapids: Zondervan, 1981), 9:148.

8. R. V. G. Tasker, *The Gospel according to St. John: An Introduction and Commentary* (Grand Rapids: Eerdmans, 1960), 181.

9. For example, James Montgomery Boice, *The Gospel of John: An Expositional Commentary* (Grand Rapids: Zondervan, 1978), 4:296–301; Frederic Louis Godet, *Commentary on John's Gospel* (reprint, Grand Rapids: Kregel, 1978), 872; and John MacArthur, *The MacArthur Study Bible* (Nashville: Word, 1997), 1617.

10. For example, Godet, *Commentary on John's Gospel,* 872; and Hendriksen, *Exposition of the Gospel according to John,* 329, 345.

11. Lindars, *The Gospel of John,* 505.

12. Barnes, *Barnes' Notes on the New Testament,* 348; C. K. Barrett, *The Gospel according to St. John,* 2d ed. (Philadelphia: Westminster, 1978), 490; Marcus Dods, "The Gospel of St. John," in *The Expositor's Greek Testament,* 1:835; Morris, *The Gospel according to John,* 701; Swete, *The Holy Spirit in the New Testament,* 163; and Westcott, *The Gospel according to St. John,* 231.

13. Tasker, *The Gospel according to St. John,* 181–82. *The NIV Study Bible* says this phrase "probably means the whole Christian way or revelation (presented and preserved in the apostolic writings), still

future at the time Christ spoke" (*The NIV Study Bible,* ed. Kenneth Barker [Grand Rapids: Zondervan, 1985], 1628).

14. John F. Walvoord, "How Can Man Know God?" *Bibliotheca Sacra* 116 (April–June 1959): 106–7.

15. F. W. Grosheide suggests that "the deep things of God" (2:10) are the same as "the things of God" (2:11), which are "God Himself in His infinitude" (*Commentary on the First Epistle to the Corinthians,* New International Commentary on the New Testament [Grand Rapids: Eerdmans, 1953], 68).

CHAPTER 4—MINISTRIES OF THE SPIRIT
RELATED TO TEACHING

1. Excellent discussions on the necessity of biblical inerrancy are given in these works: Stewart Custer, *Does Inspiration Demand Inerrancy?* (Nutley, N.J.: Craig, 1968); Norman L. Geisler, ed., *Inerrancy* (Grand Rapids: Zondervan, 1979); John Warwick Montgomery, ed., *God's Inerrant Word* (Minneapolis: Bethany House, 1974); and Charles C. Ryrie, *What You Should Know about Inerrancy* (Chicago: Moody, 1981).

2. J. I. Packer, *"Fundamentalism" and the Word of God* (Grand Rapids: Eerdmans, 1958), 111–12.

3. Henry Wheeler Robinson, *The Christian Experience of the Holy Spirit* (London: Nisbet, 1928), 182.

4. L. Gaussen, *The Inspiration of the Holy Scriptures* (Chicago: Moody, 1949), 118–23.

5. Walter Bauer, William F. Arndt, and F. Wilbur Gingrich, *A Greek-English Lexicon of the New Testament and Other Early Christian Literature,* 2d ed., rev. F. Wilbur Gingrich and Frederick W. Danker (Chicago: University of Chicago Press, 1979), 248.

6. Julius Charles Hare, *The Mission of the Comforter,* 2d ed. (Boston: Gould & Lincoln, 1854), 348–55, note K.

7. John Calvin, *Institutes of the Christian Religion,* trans. John Allen (Grand Rapids: Eerdmans, 1949), 1.7.4.

8. *Chicago Statement on Biblical Inerrancy* (Oakland, Calif.: International Council on Biblical Inerrancy, 1978), para. 3.

9. For example, Walvoord, *The Holy Spirit,* 112.

10. Lewis Sperry Chafer, *Systematic Theology*, 8 vols. in 4 (Grand Rapids: Kregel, 1993), 3:322.

11. Kenneth S. Wuest, *The Practical Use of the Greek New Testament* (Chicago: Moody, 1946), 152.

12. F. F. Bruce, *The Epistles of John* (Old Tappan, N.J.: Revell, 1970), 71-72; and Raymond E. Brown, *The Epistles of John*, Anchor Bible (Garden City, N.Y.: Doubleday, 1982), 348–49, 369–70.

13. Alfred Plummer, *The Epistles of St. John, with Notes, Introduction, and Appendices* (Cambridge: University Press, 1886), 61.

14. Brooke Foss Westcott, *The Epistles of St. John: The Greek Text with Notes and Essays* (London: Macmillan, 1883), 72.

15. Abraham Kuyper, *The Work of the Holy Spirit* (Grand Rapids: Eerdmans, 1956), 185.

16. Bruce, *The Epistles of John*, 76.

17. Robertson, *Word Pictures in the New Testament*, 6:218.

18. R. C. H. Lenski, *The Interpretation of the Epistles of St. Peter and St. Jude* (Minneapolis: 1961), 442.

19. Henry Alford, *The Greek Testament*, rev. ed., 4 vols. in 2 (Chicago: Moody, 1958), 4:455.

20. Kenneth S. Wuest, *In These Last Days* (Grand Rapids: Eerdmans, 1957), 138.

21. Howard Marshall, *The Epistles of John* (Grand Rapids: Eerdmans, 1978), 163.

22. Albert Benjamin Simpson, *The Holy Spirit* (New York: Christian Alliance, 1895), 2:324–5.

23. Brown, *The Epistles of John*, 374–76.

24. Donald W. Burdick, *The Epistles of John* (Chicago: Moody, 1970), 47.

25. Joseph Henry Thayer, *A Greek-English Lexicon of the New Testament*, 4th ed. (Edinburgh: Clark, 1901), 663.

26. Calvin, *Institutes of the Christian Religion*, 3.2.34.

27. Edwin H. Palmer, *The Holy Spirit* (Grand Rapids: Baker, 1958), 59.

28. Kuyper, *The Work of the Holy Spirit*, 76.

29. Fred H. Klooster, "The Role of the Holy Spirit in the Hermeneutic Process" (paper presented at the Chicago Summit Conference II,

International Council on Biblical Inerrancy, Oakland, Calif., 1982),
3, 6, 14–17.

30. Geoffrey W. Bromiley, "The Bible Doctrine of Inspiration," *Christianity Today,* 23 November 1959, 139 (italics added).
31. Klooster, "The Role of the Holy Spirit in the Hermeneutic Process," 16.
32. Walvoord, "How Can Man Know God?" 105.
33. Daniel F. Fuller, "Do We Need the Holy Spirit to Understand the Bible?" *Eternity* (January 1959): 22.
34. Henry A. Virkler, *Hermeneutics: Principles and Processes of Biblical Interpretation* (Grand Rapids: Baker, 1981), 30 (italics his).
35. Charles Hodge, *Systematic Theology* (Grand Rapids: Eerdmans, 1960), 3:403.
36. Arthur W. Lindsley, "A Response to 'The Role of the Holy Spirit in the Hermeneutic Process,'" (paper presented at the Chicago Summit Conference II, International Council on Biblical Inerrancy, Oakland, Calif., 1982), 3.
37. J. Theodore Mueller, "The Holy Spirit and the Scriptures," in *Revelation and the Bible,* 280.
38. Randolph Crump Miller, "The Holy Spirit and Christian Education," *Religious Education* 57 (May/June 1962): 178 (italics his).

CHAPTER 5—FALSE VIEWS ON
THE DIVINE AND HUMAN TEACHERS

1. Geoffrey F. Outtalk, *The Holy Spirit in Puritan Faith and Experience* (Oxford: Blackwell, 1946), 83–85.
2. LeBar, *Education That Is Christian,* 239.
3. Edge, *Teaching for Results,* 19.
4. Clarence H. Benson, *The Christian Teacher* (Chicago: Moody, 1950), 13 (italics added).
5. Ibid., 63.
6. Ibid., 64.
7. Edge, *Teaching for Results,* 20.
8. LeBar, *Education That Is Christian,* 239.

CHAPTER 6—WHAT IS THE GIFT OF TEACHING?

1. John F. Walvoord says at least sixteen spiritual gifts are mentioned in the New Testament (*The Holy Spirit,* 168). Leslie B. Flynn lists nineteen. *Nineteen Gifts of the Spirit* [Wheaton, Ill.: Victor, 1974], 28-36). And William J. McRae discusses twenty (*The Dynamics of Spiritual Gifts* [Grand Rapids: Zondervan, 1976], 43–45).

2. Charles Caldwell Ryrie, *Biblical Theology of the New Testament* (Chicago: Moody, 1959), 178.

3. Walvoord, *The Holy Spirit,* 165–66.

4. McRae, *The Dynamics of Spiritual Gifts,* 36.

5. Walvoord, *The Holy Spirit,* 173–88.

6. McRae, *The Dynamics of Spiritual Gifts,* 90–99; Joseph Dillow, *Speaking in Tongues* (Grand Rapids: Zondervan, 1975); Robert G. Gromacki, *The Modern Tongues Movement* (Nutley, N. J.: Presbyterian and Reformed, 1973); and Robert P. Lightner, *Speaking in Tongues and Divine Healing,* 2d ed. (Schaumburg, Ill.: Regular Baptist, 1978). Also see comments on 1 Corinthians 13:8–13 and 14:20–22 by David K. Lowery, "1 Corinthians," in *The Bible Knowledge Commentary, New Testament,* ed. John F. Walvoord and Roy B. Zuck (Wheaton, Ill.: Victor, 1983), 535–37, 539.

7. George Barker Stevens, *The Theology of the New Testament,* 2d ed. (Edinburgh: Clark, 1918), 434.

8. For discussion on the relationship between teaching and preaching see my book *Teaching as Paul Taught* (Grand Rapids: Baker, 1998), 28–40.

9. For more on Paul's teaching ministry see Zuck, *Teaching as Paul Taught.*

10. Walvoord, *The Holy Spirit,* 176.

11. R. C. H. Lenski, *The Interpretation of St. Paul's First and Second Epistles to the Corinthians* (Minneapolis: Augsburg, 1961), 490.

12. Lindsay Dewar, *The Holy Spirit and Modern Thought* (New York: Harper & Row, 1959), 67.

13. Walvoord, *The Holy Spirit,* 75.

14. Ibid., 167.

15. McRae, *The Dynamics of Spiritual Gifts,* 49.

16. Frank E. Gaebelein, *The Pattern of God's Truth* (New York: Oxford University Press, 1954), 20.
17. Ibid., 23.
18. Henry T. Blackaby and Claude V. King seem to suggest that a spiritual gift is not a permanent possession but is more of a carrying out of a God-given "assignment" (*Experiencing God* [Nashville: Broadman & Holman, 1994], 48–49).
19. Barnes, *Barnes' Notes on the New Testament,* 1169.
20. Charles Caldwell Ryrie, "The Pauline Doctrine of the Church," *Bibliotheca Sacra* 115 (January–March 1958): 64.
21. Flynn, *Nineteen Gifts of the Spirit,* 80.

CHAPTER 7—DISTINCTIVE MINISTIRES OF THE DIVINE AND HUMAN TEACHERS

1. Harold C. Mason, *The Teaching Task of the Local Church* (Winona Lake, Ind.: Light and Life, 1960), 22.
2. Gilbert A. Peterson, "The Christian Teacher," in *Introduction to Biblical Christian Education*, 83.
3. LeBar, *Education That Is Christian,* 246.
4. Augustus Hopkins Strong, *Systematic Theology* (Philadelphia: Judson, 1907), 27.
5. LeBar, *Education That Is Christian,* 250–51.
6. Walter C. Kaiser, Jr., *Toward an Exegetical Theology: Biblical Exegesis for Teaching and Preaching* (Grand Rapids: Baker, 1981), 236.
7. Gaebelein, *Christian Education in a Democracy,* 279.
8. Benson, *The Christian Teacher*, 50.
9. Earle E. Cairns, "The Essence of Christian Higher Education," *Bibliotheca Sacra* 111 (October–December 1954): 344–45.

CHAPTER 8—THE BIBLE AS THE AUTHORITY FOR CHRISTIAN EDUCATION

1. Packer, *"Fundamentalism" and the Word of God,* 42.
2. Joseph Foa Di Bruno, *Catholic Belief,* 2d ed. (London: Burns & Oates, 1878), 24.

3. Bernard Ramm, *The Witness of the Spirit* (Grand Rapids: Eerdmans, 1959), 11–12.

4. John Calvin, *The Deity of Christ and Other Sermons,* trans. LeRoy Nixon (Grand Rapids: Eerdmans, 1950), 243.

5. Calvin, *Institutes of the Christian Religion,* 1.7.1.

6. Packer, *"Fundamentalism" and the Word of God,* 113.

7. John Dewey, *Experience and Education* (New York: Macmillan, 1938), 4–5.

8. LeBar, *Education That Is Christian,* 180 (italics hers).

9. John Dewey, *Democracy and Education* (Darby, Pa.: Darby, 1932), 169.

10. Ibid., 415.

11. Kenneth O. Gangel, "John Dewey: An Evangelical Evaluation," *Bibliotheca Sacra 124* (January–March 1967): 29.

12. Dewey, *Experience and Education,* 17.

13. For a helpful overview of Dewey's philosophy and educational principles, see David H. Roper, "John Dewey," in *A History of Religious Educators,* ed. Elmer L. Towns (Grand Rapids: Baker, 1975), 310-26.

14. Charles E. S. Kraemer, "Relating Revelation to Education," *Presbyterian Action* (April 1958): 6.

15. Harrison S. Elliott, *Can Religious Education Be Christian?* (New York: Macmillan, 1949), 320.

16. Bernard Ramm, *The Pattern of Authority* (Grand Rapids: Eerdmans, 1957), 76.

17. Auguste Sabatier, *Religions of Authority and the Religion of the Spirit,* trans. L. S. Houghton (New York: McClure, 1904), 264.

18. Millar Burrows, *An Outline of Biblical Theology* (Philadelphia: Westminster, 1945), 50.

19. Balmer H. Kelly, "The Bible Is Witness and Instrument," *Presbyterian Action* (April 1958): 10–11.

20. Karl Barth, *The Holy Ghost and the Christian Life,* trans. R. Birch Hoyle (London: Muller, 1938), 39.

21. George H. Schreyer, *Christian Education in Theological Focus* (Philadelphia: Christian Education, 1962), 55 (italics his).

22. Ibid., 56.

23. Rachel Henderlite, *The Holy Spirit in Christian Education* (Philadelphia: Westminster, 1964), 62, 67.

24. Ibid., 67.

25. Ibid., 72, 77, 119.

26. Ibid., 59.

27. Ibid., 79.

28. Ibid.

29. R. A. Finlayson, "Contemporary Views of Inspiration," in *Revelation and the Bible*, 30.

30. Bernard Ramm has attempted to defend much of Barthian theology by suggesting that it is not so distant from evangelicalism as many evangelicals previously supposed. However, Ramm still admits that Karl Barth makes a distinction or "an interval between the Word of God and the text of Holy Scripture" *(After Fundamentalism* [San Francisco: Harper & Row, 1983], 89).

31. Schreyer, in fact, says that helping persons in their "responses toward encounters with God" is the goal of Christian education (Schreyer, *Christian Education in Theological Focus*, 8).

32. William Temple, *Nature, Men, and God* (New York: Macmillan, 1949), 353.

33. J. I. Packer, "Contemporary Views of Revelation," in *Revelation and the Bible*, 95.

34. Herbert H. Framer, "The Bible: Its Significance and Authority," in *The Interpreter's Bible*, ed. George A. Buttrick (Nashville: Abingdon, 1952), 1:24.

35. Lewis Howard Grimes, "Christianity Is Learned through Living Encounter with the Bible," in *The Minister and Christian Nurture*, ed. Nathaniel Frederick Forsyth (New York: Abingdon, 1957), 152.

36. George Park Fisher, *History of Christian Doctrine* (Edinburgh: Clark, 1949), 11.

37. Packer, *"Fundamentalism" and the Word of God*, 61–62.

38. Ramm, *The Pattern of Authority*, 36.

39. Ibid., p. 28.

40. J. N. Thomas, "The Authority of the Bible," *Theology Today* 3 (July 1946): 166 (italics his).

41. Finlayson, "Contemporary Views of Inspiration," 233.

42. Grimes, "Christianity Is Learned through Living Encounter with the Bible," 144.

43. LeBar, *Education That Is Christian*, 19.

CHAPTER 9—THE BIBLE AS THE BASIC
CONTENT OF CHRISTIAN EDUCATION

1. William Clayton Bower, "Religious Education Faces the Future," *Journal of Religion* 21 (October 1941): 389.
2. George Albert Coe, *What Is Christian Education?* (New York: Scribner, 1929), chapter 3.
3. Ludwig Haetzer, quoted in Wiswedel, "Bible: Inner and Outer Word," 326.
4. Edward L. Hayes, "The Centrality of the Bible in Christian Education," *Bibliotheca Sacra* 126 (July–September 1969): 231.
5. D. Campbell Wyckoff, *The Gospel and Christian Education* (Philadelphia: Westminster, 1959), 92.
6. Sara Little, *The Role of the Bible in Contemporary Christian Education* (Richmond, Va.: Knox, 1961), 156.
7. Manuel Flores, "Biblical Theology in Christian Education," *World Christian Education* 16 (third quarter, 1961): 76.
8. For more detail on the neoorthodox view of Christian education, see these articles of mine: "The Theological Bases of Neoorthodox Christian Education," *Bibliotheca Sacra* 119 (April–June 1962): 161–69; and "The Educational Pattern of Neoorthodox Christian Education," *Bibliotheca Sacra* 119 (October–December 1962): 342–51.

CHAPTER 10—THE HOLY SPIRIT AND
BIBLICAL INTERPRETATION

1. H. C. G. Moule, *Veni Creator: Thoughts on the Person and Work of the Holy Spirit of Promise* (London: Stoughton, 1890), 63.
2. Joseph Parker, *The Paraclete* (1874; reprint, New York: Scribner, Armstrong, 1975), 78.
3. A. Berkeley Mickelsen, *Interpreting the Bible* (Grand Rapids: Eerdmans, 1963), 5. Also see my book, *Basic Bible Interpretation* (Wheaton, Ill.: Victor, 1991), 19–20.

4. Bernard Ramm, *Protestant Biblical Interpretation*, 3d ed. (Grand Rapids: Baker, 1970), 13.

5. Ibid., 13–14.

6. John McClintock and James Strong, *Cyclopedia of Biblical, Theological, and Ecclesiastical Literature* (reprint, Grand Rapids: Baker, 1959), 4:205.

7. Mickelsen, *Interpreting the Bible*, 39.

8. Parker, *The Paraclete*, 83.

9. Chafer, *He That Is Spiritual*, 62.

10. Klooster, "The Role of the Holy Spirit in the Hermeneutic Process," 12–13.

11. Ramm, *Protestant Biblical Interpretation*, 17.

12. Ibid.

13. Ibid.

14. Chafer, *Systematic Theology*, 1:vi.

15. See Norman L. Geisler, "The Concept of Truth in the Contemporary Inerrancy Debate," *Bibliotheca Sacra* 137 (October–December 1980): 327–39.

16. Ramm, *The Pattern of Authority*, 37.

17. Zuck, *Basic Bible Interpretation*, 15–18. Also see Robert T. Sandin, "The Clarity of Scripture," in *The Living and Active Word of God: Studies in Honor of Samuel J. Schultz*, ed. Morris Inch and Ronald Youngblood (Winona Lake, Ind.: Eisenbrauns, 1983), 240–41.

18. Klooster, "The Role of the Holy Spirit in the Hermeneutic Process," 14.

19. James Michael Lee, "The Authentic Source of Religious Instruction," in *Religious Education and Theology*, ed. Norma H. Thompson (Birmingham, Ala.: Religious Education, 1982), 194.

20. Ibid., 195.

21. Ibid., 196–97.

22. Ibid., 193–94.

23. Lee, "Toward a New Era: A Blueprint for Positive Action," 130.

PART 4—THE HOLY SPIRIT IN
THE TEACHING-LEARNING PROCESS

1. Benson, *The Christian Teacher*, 209.

CHAPTER 11—PRINCIPLES OF LEARNING
AND THE WORK OF THE HOLY SPIRIT

1. C. B. Eavey, *Principles of Teaching for Christian Teachers* (Grand Rapids: Zondervan, 1940), 46.

2. Roy B. Zuck, "Application in Biblical Hermeneutics and Exposition," in *Walvoord: A Tribute*, ed. Donald K. Campbell (Chicago: Moody, 1982), 16.

3. R. C. H. Lenski, *The Interpretation of St. Paul's Epistles to the Colossians, to the Thessalonians, to Timothy, to Titus, and to Philemon* (Minneapolis: Augsburg, 1961), 847.

4. James DeForest Murch, *Christian Education and the Local Church*, rev. ed. (Cincinnati: Standard, 1943), 100.

5. Blackaby and King, *Experiencing God*, 50–62.

6. Ronald P. Chadwick, *Teaching and Learning* (Old Tappan, N.J.: Revell, 1982), 27–32; Edward L. Hayes, "The Biblical Foundations of Christian Education," in *Introduction to Biblical Christian Education*, 32; Ian A. Muirhead, *Education in the New Testament* (New York: Association, 1965), especially chapters 1–3; Roy B. Zuck, "Hebrew Words for Teach," *Bibliotheca Sacra* 121 (July–September 1964): 228–35; Roy B. Zuck, "Greek Words for Teach," *Bibliotheca Sacra* 122 (April–June 1965): 158–68; Roy B. Zuck, *Teaching as Jesus Taught* (Grand Rapids: Baker, 1995), 92–96; and Zuck, *Teaching as Paul Taught*, 28–40.

7. Robert F. Mager, *Preparing Instructional Objectives* (Palo Alto, Calif.: Fearon, 1962); *Developing Attitude toward Learning* (Palo Alto, Calif.: Fearon, 1968); and *Measuring Instructional Intent* (Palo Alto, Calif.: Fearon, 1973).

8. LeRoy Ford, "Developing Performance-Oriented Learning Purposes," *Search* 4 (Winter 1974): 31–40.

9. David R. Krathwohl, Benjamin S. Bloom, and Bertram B. Masia, *Taxonomy of Educational Objectives, Handbook II: Affective Domain* (New York: McKay, 1904).

10. LeBar, *Education That Is Christian*, 228.

11. Dennis H. Dirks, "The Teacher: Facilitator for Change," in *Christian Education: Foundations for the Future*, ed. Robert E. Clark, Lin Johnson, and Allyn K. Sloat (Chicago: Moody, 1991), 139.

12. Henderlite, *The Holy Spirit in Christian Education*, 36, 80–82; Howard Crimes, "Theological Foundations for Christian Education," in *An Introduction to Christian Education*, ed. Marvin J. Taylor (Nashville: Abingdon, 1966), 36.

13. Zuck, "The Educational Program of Neoorthodox Christian Education," 348 (italics in original).

14. LeBar, *Education That Is Christian*, 142–43.

15. Thom Schultz and Joani Schultz, *Why Nobody Learns Much of Anything at Church: And How to Fix It* (Loveland, Colo.: Group, 1993), 29.

16. Paul H. Vieth, *Teaching for Christian Living*, 3d ed. (St. Louis: Bethany, 1929), 97–98.

17. Paul H. Vieth, ed., *The Church and Christian Education* (St. Louis: Bethany, 1947), 74–75.

18. Bauer, Arndt, and Gingrich, *A Greek-English Lexicon of the New Testament and Other Early Christian Literature*, 491.

19. Ruth Beechick, *A Biblical Psychology of Learning: How Your Mind Works* (Denver: Accent, 1982); Robert R. Boehlke, *Theories of Learning in Christian Education* (Philadelphia: Westminster, 1962); Edge, *Teaching for Results*, 15–31; Milford H. Henkel, "The Learning Process for Adults," in *Adult Education in the Local Church*, ed. Roy B. Zuck and Gene A. Getz (Chicago: Moody, 1970), 100–117; Donald M. Joy, *Meaningful Learning in the Church* (Winona Lake, Ind.: Light and Life, 1969); and Charles R. Stinnett, Jr., *Learning in Theological Perspective* (New York: Association, 1965).

20. J. L. Corzine, *Looking at Learning* (Nashville: Sunday School Board, 1934), 81.

21. Ibid., 80.

22. Edge, *Teaching for Results*, 25.

23. G. Lester Anderson, "Basic Learning Theory for Teachers," in *Educational Psychology,* ed. Charles E. Skinner, 4th ed. (Englewood Cliffs, N.J.: Prentice-Hall, 1959), 406.

24. Howard Mayes and James Long, *Can I Help It If They Don't Learn?* (Wheaton, Ill.: Victor Books, 1977), 17.

25. Ibid.

26. See my list of sixty needs Paul addressed in his epistles (Zuck, *Teaching as Paul Taught,* 145–46).

27. LeBar, *Education That Is Christian,* 154.

28. Lawrence O. Richards, *Creative Bible Teaching* (Chicago: Moody, 1970), 135.

29. Kenneth O. Gangel, "Integrating Faith and Learning: Principles and Process," *Bibliotheca Sacra* 135 (April–June 1978): 108.

30. Mayes and Long, *Can I Help It If They Don't Learn?* 32–47, 67–84.

31. Schultz and Schultz, *Why Nobody Learns Much of Anything at Church: And How to Fix It,* 105–39.

32. Zuck, *Teaching as Jesus Taught,* 174.

33. Henkel, "The Learning Process for Adults," 113.

34. Joy, *Meaningful Learning in the Church,* 55.

35. Charles A. Trentham, "Knowledge and the Holy Spirit," *Baptist Student* (April 1957): 31.

36. Chafer, *Systematic Theology,* 1:113.

37. S. A. Witmer, "Enduring Foundations in Education: The Other John," *United Evangelical Action,* 15 June 1955, 224.

38. For extensive discussions on how people learn, written from a Christian perspective, see Daniel L. Barlow, *Educational Psychology: The Teaching-Learning Process* (Chicago: Moody, 1985); and Klaus Issler and Ronald Habermass, *How We Learn: A Christian Teacher's Guide to Educational Psychology* (Grand Rapids: Baker, 1994).

CHAPTER 12—TEACHING METHODOLOGY AND THE WORK OF THE HOLY SPIRIT

1. John Milton Gregory, *The Seven Laws of Teaching* (Grand Rapids: Baker, 1955), 2.

2. Edge, *Teaching for Results*, 223 (italics his).

3. Zuck, *Teaching as Paul Taught*, 6–109.

4. Richard Osberg, "The Christian Teacher's Authentic Person," *Journal of Christian Education* 1 (Spring 1981): 53.

5. Some recommended books are these: Werner C. Graendorf, ed., *Introduction to Biblical Christian Education*, chapters 9–11; Clark, Johnson, and Sloat, *Christian Education: Foundations for the Future*, chapters 15–21; Roy B. Zuck and Warren S. Benson, eds., *Youth Education in the Church* (Chicago: Moody, 1978), chapters 8–10; Robert E. Clark, Joanne Brubaker, and Roy B. Zuck, eds., *Childhood Education in the Church*, rev. ed. (Chicago: Moody, 1975), chapters 3–10; Zuck and Getz, eds., *Adult Education in the Church*, chapters 3–6; and Michael J. Anthony, ed., *Foundations of Ministry* (Wheaton, Ill.: Scripture Press, 1992), chapters 9–11, 13.

6. Edge, *Teaching for Results*, 21.

7. Carl J. Moses, "The Most Important Characteristic of an Effective Teacher," *Journal of Christian Education* 2 (1981): 51–55.

8. Ronald C. Doll, "Shall We Close the Sunday Schools?" *Christianity Today*, 31 August 1959, 4.

9. Chafer, *He That Is Spiritual*, 63.

10. Clarice M. Bowman, *Ways Youth Learn* (New York: Harper & Row, 1952), 8.

11. Robert S. Traina, *Methodical Bible Study* (Grand Rapids: Francis Asbury, 1985), 19.

12. L. Nelson Bell, "Teaching—Methods and Message," *Christianity Today*, 29 August 1960, 25.

13. Among the books that discuss these and other methods, these are recommended: Findley B. Edge, *Helping the Learner* (Nashville: Broadman, 1959), 69–181; LeRoy Ford, *Using the Lecture in Teaching and Training* (Nashville: Broadman,1968), 5; Kenneth O. Gangel, *Twenty-Four Ways to Improve Your Teaching* (Wheaton, Ill.: Victor, 1971); William B. Haburn, "Methods in Teaching," in *Introduction to Biblical Christian Education*, 178–87; Marlene D. LeFever, "Creative Methods," in *Youth Education in the Church*, 406–21; Marlene D. LeFever, *Creative Teaching Methods* (Elgin, Ill.: David C. Cook,

1985), 63–320; J. Omar Brubaker, "Instructional Methodology for Adults," in *Adult Education in the Church,* 118–42; Richards, *Creative Bible Teaching;* Norris M. Sanders, *Classroom Questions* (New York: Harper & Row, 1966); and Clark, Brubaker, and Zuck, eds., *Childhood Education in the Church,* chapters 27–32.

On Jesus' methods of teaching see these works: Donald Guthrie, "Jesus," in *A History of Religious Educators,* 15–38; Herman Harrell Horne, *Teaching Techniques of Jesus* (Grand Rapids: Kregel, 1974); LeBar, *Education That Is Christian,* chapter 3, "The Teacher Come from God"; J. M. Price, *Jesus the Teacher* (Nashville: Convention, 1946); Clifford A. Wilson, *Jesus the Master Teacher* (Grand Rapids: Baker, 1974); Valerie A. Wilson, "Christ the Master Teacher," in *Introduction to Biblical Christian Education,* 54–67; and Zuck, *Teaching as Jesus Taught,* 165–81.

14. Rice A. Pierce, *Leading Dynamic Bible Study* (Nashville: Broadman, 1969), 117 (italics his).

15. LeBar, *Education That Is Christian,* 227.

16. Carl F. H. Henry, "Pastors and Christian Education," *Christianity Today,* 31 August 1959, 29. A helpful guide for evaluating curricula is given in Lawrence O. Richards, ed., *The Key to Sunday School Achievement* (Chicago: Moody, 1980), chapter 4.

17. Richards, *Creative Bible Teaching,* 142.

18. LeBar, *Education That Is Christian,* 231.

19. Ibid., 254.

PART 5—A BRIEF HISTORY OF THE HOLY SPIRIT IN TEACHING

1. For excellent surveys of the history of Christian education see Kenneth O. Gangel and Warren S. Benson, *Christian Education: Its History and Philosophy* (Chicago: Moody, 1983); D. Bruce Lockerbie, *A Passion for Learning: The History of Christian Thought on Education* (Chicago: Moody, 1994); and Towns, ed., *A History of Religious Educators.*

CHAPTER 13—THE HOLY SPIRIT AND TEACHING BEFORE THE REFORMATION

1. Henry Barclay Swete, *The Holy Spirit in the Ancient Church* (London: Macmillan, 1909), 31.

2. Francis B. Denio, *The Supreme Leader* (Boston: Pilgrim, 1900), 59.

3. Swete, *The Holy Spirit in the Ancient Church*, 25.

4. Justin Martyr, *Dialogue with Trypho* 4, quoted in Swete, *The Holy Spirit in the Ancient Church*, 34.

5. Ibid., 39, quoted in Swete, *The Holy Spirit in the Ancient Church*, 35.

6. Tertullian, *De monogamia* 2, quoted in Swete, *The Holy Spirit in the Ancient Church*, 79–80.

7. Irenaeus, *Setting Forth of the Apostolic Preaching*, quoted in Swete, *The Holy Spirit in the Ancient Church*, 87.

8. Novatian, quoted in Swete, *The Holy Spirit in the Ancient Church*, 108.

9. R. Boich Hoyle, "Spirit (Holy), Spirit of God," in *Encyclopedia of Religion and Ethics*, ed. James Hastings (New York: Scribner's Sons, n. d.), 11:802.

10. Swete, *The Holy Spirit in the Ancient Church*, 168.

11. Augustus Neander, *Lectures on the History of Christian Dogmas*, trans. J. E. Ryland (London: Bell & Daldy, 1866), 1:304.

12. C. R. B. Shapland, *The Letters of St. Athanasius concerning the Holy Spirit* (London: Epworth, 1951), 38.

13. Cyril of Jerusalem, quoted in Swete, *The Holy Spirit in the Ancient Church*, 204.

14. Augustine, quoted in Swete, *The Holy Spirit in the Ancient Church*, 334.

15. Gregory the Great, quoted in Swete, *The Holy Spirit in the Ancient Church*, 350.

16. Walvoord, *The Holy Spirit*, 244.

17. John H. S. Burleigh, *Augustine: Earlier Writings* (Philadelphia: Westminster, 1953), 95 (xi. 38).

18. Ibid.

19. Howard Grimes, "St. Augustine on Teaching," *Religious Education* 54 (March–April 1959): 173.

20. Walvoord, *The Holy Spirit*, 246.

21. Thomas Rees, *The Holy Spirit in Thought and Experience* (New York: Scribner, 1915), 176.

22. Thomas Aquinas, "Reply to Objection 7," *De Magistro*, quoted in *Basic Writings in Christian Education*, ed. Kendig Brubaker Cully, (Philadelphia: Westminster, 1960), 112.

23. Joan Ellen Dulval, "Thomas Aquinas," in *A History of Religious Educators*, 77.

24. Ibid., 76.

CHAPTER 14—THE HOLY SPIRIT AND TEACHING FROM THE REFORMATION TO THE PRESENT

1. George Smeaton, *The Doctrine of the Holy Spirit* (Edinburgh: Clark, 1882), 307.

2. Calvin, *Institutes of the Christian Religion*, 2.5.5.

3. Ibid., 1.7.5.

4. Smeaton, *The Doctrine of the Holy Spirit*, 313.

5. Regin Prenter, *Spiritus Creator*, trans. John M. Jensen (Philadelphia: Muhlenberg, 1953).

6. Ronald S. Wallace, *Calvin's Doctrine of the Word and Sacrament* (Grand Rapids: Eerdmans, 1957), 128–29.

7. Wilhelm Niesel, *The Theology of Calvin*, trans. Harold Knight (Philadelphia: Westminster, 1956), 38–39.

8. Wallace, *Calvin's Doctrine of the Word and Sacrament*, 129–30.

9. Calvin, *Institutes of the Christian Religion*, 4.16.19.

10. Ibid., 1.9.3.

11. H. Wayne Pipkin, "Ulrich Zwingli," in *A History of Religious Educators*, 131.

12. Detailed reports of the intense torture, prolonged imprisonments, and heartless executions of hundreds of Anabaptists are recorded in Thieleman J. van Braght, *Martyrs Mirror*, 10th ed. (Scottdale, Pa.: Herald, 1975), 410–1141. This book was first published in Dutch in 1660. A record of the imprisonment in 1659 and 1660 of the Swiss Anabaptist preacher Hans Zaugg, my direct ancestor, is included on pages 1124–25.

13. William R. Estep, *The Anabaptist Story*, rev. ed. (Grand Rapids: Eerdmans, 1975), 130.

14. Henry C. Vedder, *Balthasar Hubmaier* (New York: AMS, 1971), 91.

15. John C. Wenger, "The Theology of Pilgram Marpeck," *Mennonite Quarterly Review* 12 (July 1938): 214.

16. John C. Wenger, "The Schleitheim Confession of Faith," *Mennonite Quarterly Review* 19 (October 1945): 247.

17. Hans Denck, "Concerning the Law of God," quoted in Walter Klassen, ed., *Anabaptism in Outline* (Scottdale, Pa.: Herald, 1981), 73.

18. Jacob Hutter, "The Fourth Epistle of Jacob Hutter," quoted in Klassen, *Anabaptism in Outline*, 77.

19. Peter Reidemann, *Account of Our Religion, Doctrine, and Faith*, quoted in Robert Friedmann, *The Theology of Anabaptism* (Scottdale, Pa.: Herald, 1973), 55.

20. Menno Simons, "Triune God," quoted in John C. Wenger, ed., *The Complete Writings of Menno Simons* (Scottdale, Pa.: Herald, 1956), 496.

21. Dirk Philips, "The Church of God," quoted in Klassen, *Anabaptism in Outline*, 82.

22. Benjamin B. Warfield, "Introductory Note," in Abraham Kuyper, *The Work of the Holy Spirit*, trans. Henri DeVries (Grand Rapids: Eerdmans, 1956), xxxiii.

23. Geoffrey F. Nuttall, *The Holy Spirit in Puritan Faith and Experience* (Oxford: Blackwell, 1946), 83–85.

24. Robert Barlay, quoted in *Documents of the Christian Church*, ed. Henry Bettenson (New York: Oxford University Press, 1954), 355.

25. Howard Watkin-Jones, *The Holy Spirit from Arminius to Wesley* (London: Epworth, 1929), 186.

26. Gangel and Benson, *Christian Education: Its History and Philosophy*, 172–76.

27. Paul Beck, *The Memoirs of August Hermann Francke* (Philadelphia: American Sunday School Union, 1831), 149.

28. Horace Bushnell, *Christian Nurture* (reprint, New Haven, Conn.: Yale University Press, 1966), 166–67.

29. Horace Bushnell, *Sermons for the New Life* (New York: Scribner, 1867), 108–9.

30. George Albert Coe, *What Is Christian Education?* (New York: Scribner, 1929), 33.

31. Gaebelein, *Christian Education in a Democracy*, 219.

32. James D. Smart, *The Teaching Ministry of the Church* (Philadelphia: Westminster, 1954), 63.

33. Karl Barth, *The Holy Ghost and the Christian Life*, trans. R. Birch Hoyle (London: Muller, 1938), 45.

34. Elliott, *Can Religious Education Be Christian?*, 72.

35. Ibid., 73.

36. George A. Coe, "Religious Education Is in Peril," *International Journal of Religious Education*, 15 January 1939, 9–10.

37. Little, *The Role of the Bible in Contemporary Christian Education*, 5, 165.

38. H. Shelton Smith, *Faith and Nurture* (New York: Scribner, 1941), 244.

39. For a critique of neoliberalism, see Robert P. Lightner, *Neo-Liberalism* (Chicago: Regular Baptist, 1959).

40. Randolph Crump Miller, *The Theory of Christian Education Practice* (Birmingham: Religious Education, 1980).

41. Ibid., 34, 160. Gangel and Benson state that "existentialism is a patch-work quilt [of] such things as the transcendence of existence, the love of contradiction, the absurdity of life, extreme individualism, lack of concern for the past or the future, and an occasional patch of rank nihilism" (*Christian Education: Its History and Philosophy*, 315).

42. For evangelical critiques of postmodernism see Dennis McCallum, ed., *The Death of Truth* (Minneapolis: Bethany House, 1996); and Gene Edward Vieth, Jr., *Postmodern Times* (Wheaton, Ill.: Crossway, 1994). Also see Millard J. Erickson, *The Evangelical Left* (Grand Rapids: Baker, 1997).

CHAPTER 15—CHALLENGE: TEACH!

1. LeBar, *Education That Is Christian*, 253–54.

2. Lois E. LeBar, *Focus on People in Christian Education* (Westwood, N.J.: Revell, 1968), 24.

3. Chafer, *Systematic Theology*, 1:113.

4. LeBar, *Education That Is Christian*, 248.

5. Bell, "Teaching—Methods and Message," 25.

6. Kenneth S. Kantzer, "Calvin and the Holy Scriptures," in *Inspiration and Interpretation*, 130–37.

BIBLIOGRAPHY

Anthony, Michael J., ed. *Foundations of Ministry: An Introduction to Christian Education for a New Generation.* Wheaton, Ill.: SP Publications, 1992.

Bryan, C. Doug. *Learning to Teach, Teaching to Learn: A Holistic Approach.* Nashville: Broadman & Holman Publishers, 1993.

Chafer, Lewis Sperry. *He That Is Spiritual.* 1918. Rev. ed. Grand Rapids: Zondervan Publishing House, 1987.

Dickason, C. Fred. "The Holy Spirit in Teaching." In *Introduction to Biblical Christian Education.* Edited by Werner C. Graendorf. Chicago: Moody Press, 1981.

————. "The Holy Spirit in Education." In *Christian Education: Foundations for the Future.* Edited by Robert E. Clark, Lin Johnson, and Allyn K. Sloat. Chicago: Moody Press, 1991.

Downs, Perry G. *Teaching for Spiritual Growth.* Grand Rapids: Zondervan Publishing House, 1994.

Edge, Findley B. *Helping the Teacher.* Nashville: Broadman Publishing Co., 1959.

_____. *Teaching for Results.* Rev. ed. Nashville: Broadman Publishing Co., 1995.

Edwards, David L. "An Evaluation of Contemporary Learning Theories." In *The Christian Educator's Handbook on Teaching.* Edited by Kenneth O. Gangel and Howard G. Hendricks. Wheaton, Ill.: Victor Books, 1988.

Gangel, Kenneth O. *Twenty-Four Ways to Improve Your Teaching.* Wheaton, Ill.: Victor Books, 1971.

_____, and Warren S. Benson. *Christian Education: Its History and Philosophy.* Chicago: Moody Press, 1983.

Hare, Julius Charles. *The Mission of the Comforter.* 2d ed. Boston: Gould & Lincoln, 1854.

Hayes, Edward L. "Establishing Biblical Foundations." In *Christian Education: Foundations for the Future.* Edited by Robert E. Clark, Lin Johnson, and Allyn K. Sloat. Chicago: Moody Press, 1991.

Hendricks, Howard G. *Teaching to Change Lives.* Portland, Oreg.: Multnomah Publishing Co., 1987.

_____. *Color Outside the Lines.* Nashville: Word Publishing, 1998.

Hestenes, Roberta, Howard Hendricks, and Earl Palmer. *Mastering Teaching.* Portland, Oreg.: Multnomah Publishing Co., 1991.

Issler, Klaus, and Ronald Habermas. *Teaching for Reconciliation: Foundations and Practice of Christian Educational Ministry.* Grand Rapids: Baker Book House, 1992.

_____. *How We Learn: A Christian Teacher's Guide to Educational Psychology.* Grand Rapids: Baker Book House, 1994.

LeBar, Lois E. *Education That Is Christian.* Rev. ed. Old Tappan, N.J.: Fleming H. Revell Co., 1981.

LeFever, Marlene D. *Creative Teaching Methods.* Elgin, Ill.: David C. Cook Publishing Co., 1985.

Mayes, Howard, and James Long. *Can I Help It If They Don't Learn?* Wheaton, Ill.: Victor Books, 1977.

Packer, J. I. *Keep in Step with the Spirit.* Old Tappan, N.J.: Fleming H. Revell Co., 1984.

Pazmiño, Robert W. *Principles and Practice of Christian Education: An Evangelical Perspective.* Grand Rapids: Baker Book House, 1992.

_____. *By What Authority Do We Teach?* Grand Rapids: Baker Book House, 1994.

Richards, Lawrence O. *A Theology of Christian Education.* Grand Rapids: Zondervan Publishing House, 1975.

_____, and Gary Bredfeldt. *Creative Bible Teaching.* Rev. ed. Chicago: Moody Press, 1998.

Ryrie, Charles C. *The Holy Spirit.* Chicago: Moody Press, 1985.

Schultz, Thom, and Joani Schultz. *Why Nobody Learns Much of Anything at Church: And How to Fix It.* Loveland, Colo.: Group Publishing, 1993.

Swete, Henry Barclay. *The Holy Spirit in the New Testament.* Reprint. Grand Rapids: Baker Book House, 1976.

Swindoll, Charles R. *Flying Closer to the Flame: A Passion for the Holy Spirit.* Dallas: Word, Inc., 1993.

Walvoord, John F. *The Holy Spirit.* Rev. ed. Grand Rapids: Zondervan Publishing House, 1958.

Wilhoit, James C., and John W. Dettoni. *Nurture That Is Christian: Developmental Perspectives on Christian Education.* Wheaton, Ill.: Victor Books, 1995.

Zuck, Roy B. *Basic Bible Interpretation.* Wheaton, Ill.: Victor Books, 1991.

_____. "The Role of the Holy Spirit in Christian Teaching." In *The Christian Educator's Handbook on Teaching.* Edited by Kenneth O. Gangel and Howard G. Hendricks. Wheaton, Ill.: Victor Books, 1991.

_____. *Teaching as Jesus Taught.* Grand Rapids: Baker Book House, 1995.

_____. *Teaching as Paul Taught.* Grand Rapids: Baker Book House, 1998.

SCRIPTURE INDEX

SUBJECT INDEX

Cyril of Jerusalem, 15, 141

—D—

Demosthenes, 15
Denck, Hans, 148
Dewar, Lindsay, 62
Dewey, John, 83, 84, 124, 152, 153
Dialogue with Trypho, 140
Dickason, C. Fred, 18
Dillow, Joseph, 59
Dirks, Dennis H., 114
Doll, Ronald C., 130
Duns Scotus, 143
Dutch Anabaptists, 149

—E—

Ecclesiasticism, 150
Eckhart, Johannes, 143
Edge, Findley, 5, 53, 119, 127, 128
Edification, 60
Education, Christian.
    See Christian education
Educational theory, 84–86.
    See also Dewey, John
Edwards, Jonathan, 150
Elliott, Harrison, 154
Epiphanius, 15
Eunomius, 141
Evangelicalism
    on Holy Spirit's teaching
        ministry, 156
Existential encounter
    in education, 86–87
Experience
    role in Christian education, 95–96

—F—

Faith and Nurture, 155
Finlayson, R. A., 87
Finney, Charles, 150
Fisher, George, 89
Flores, Manuel, 99
Ford, LeRoy, 113

Fox, George, 150
Framer, Herbert, 89
Francke, August Hermann, 150

—G—

Gaebelein, Frank, 64–65, 153
Gangel, Kenneth O., 120
Gaussen, L., 34
Gift of teaching, 57–69, 72
    developing gift, 66–67
    discerning gift, 65–66, 68–69
    educational technique and, 67–68,
        69
    function, 65–69
    natural vs. supernatural, 61–65
    nature of gift, 60–65
    other gifts and, 57–60.
    See also Christian education;
        Christian teacher;
        Learning; Power in teaching;
        Teaching methodology, Holy
        Spirit and
God. *See* Holy Spirit; Jesus Christ
Grebel, Conrad, 147
Gregory, John, 127
Gregory Nazianzen, 141
Gregory of Nyssa, 15, 141
Gregory the Great, 142
Grimes, Howard, 142
Grimes, Lewis, 89
Gromacki, Robert G., 59
Guidance
    of Holy Spirit, 25–27

—H—

Haetzer, Ludwig, 95
Hayes, Edward, 97
Helvetic Confession, 146
Henderlite, Rachel, 86
Hermeneutics, 102, 103
    Holy Spirit in, 106–7
Hilary of Poitiers, 141
Hildegard, 143

Hodge, 44
Holy Spirit
  as Counselor, 12
  as paraclete, 14–17
  as spirit of counsel and power, 13
  as spirit of knowledge and fear of
    Lord, 12, 13
  as Spirit of truth, 12, 13–14
  as Spirit of wisdom and revelation,
    12, 17–18
  Bible interpretation and, 101–8
  Bible study and, 7–9, 51–52.
  See also Holy Spirit as teacher;
  Teaching methodology, Holy Spirit
    and
Holy Spirit as teacher, 6–9, 160–61
  channel in teaching, 72–73
  curriculum and, 55–56, 132–34
  false views, 51–56
  human effort and, 52–54
  humanism and, 150–51
  motivation to learn and, 118–19
  principles of learning and, 111–24
  "spiritual footnote" idea, 54
  teaching methodology and, 127–34
  teaching ministries of, 21–30
  teaching–related ministries, 31–47
  titles in the Bible, 11–12
  vs. human teachers, 71–77
  Word of God and, 73–77.
  See also Holy Spirit, historical
  views on teaching ministry;
  Holy Spirit, teaching ministries of
Holy Spirit, historical views on
    teaching ministry
  Anabaptist, 147–49
  ante–Nicene, 139–40
  Calvin, 146
  evangelicalism, 156
  inspirationist, 147–48
  liberal, 152–53, 155
  Luther, 146
  Middle Ages, 142–43
  modern, 151–56

  Nicene, 141–42
  neoorthodoxy, 153–54
  Pietist, 150
  post–Nicene, 141–42
  post–Reformation, 149–51
  Puritan, 149
  Reformation, 145–49
  Revivalism, 150.
  See also Holy Spirit, teaching
    ministries of
Holy Spirit, teaching ministries of,
    21–30
  declaring, 27–28
  guiding, 25–27
  instruction, 22–24
  reminding, 25
  revelation, 29–30.
  See also Holy Spirit, teaching–
    related ministries of
  Teaching methodology, Holy Spirit
    and
Holy Spirit, teaching–related
    ministries of, 31–46
  conviction, 34–35
  divine teaching, 33
  illumination, 40–46
  indwelling, 35–39
  inspiration, 31–34
Hubmaier, Balthasar, 148
Hugo of St. Victor, 143
Humanism
  on Holy Spirit's teaching ministry,
    150–51
Hutter, Jacob, 148

—I—

Ignatius, 139
Illumination by Holy Spirit, 40–46
  perception vs. reception, 42
  relation to Bible, 41–42
  vs. interpretation, 107
Indwelling of Holy Spirit, 35–39
Inerrancy of Bible. *See* Bible, as
  inerrant

198